PARACORD FUSION TIES

VOLUME 1

Straps, Slip Knots, Falls, Bars, & Bundles

PARACORD FUSION TIES

VOLUME 1

Straps, Slip Knots, Falls, Bars, & Bundles

Written & Photographed by
JD of *Tying It All Together*

4th Level Indie

Fusion Ties – Innovative ties created through the merging of different knot elements or knotting techniques.

Paracord Fusion Ties - Volume 1
by J.D. Lenzen
ISBN: 978-0-9855578-0-5

Published by *4th Level Indie*
Author's Site: fusionknots.com

Printed in the United States by BPR Book Group.

Massively distributed by Itasca Books Distribution.

Contents

Foreword

I grew up as an Army brat and spent some time in the Boy Scouts. So I'm not a complete stranger to rope ties and knotwork. But it wasn't until I was an adult that I found a knot book on the discount shelf of a bookstore and, thumbing through it, noticed instructions for how to tie a Crown Sinnet. Up to that point, I had only occasionally seen elaborate knots, primarily tied around small items, like pocket knives and flashlights (which I've always had a fascination for). But a building curiosity drove me to search for other books and online resources that provided more examples of decorative knots and instructions for how to tie them. In time, I started blogging about my addiction to decorative and useful knotwork, creating Stormdrane's Blog in April of 2005.

The search for new ties is unending. Because with knot tying, braiding, and weaving, the more you know, the more you discover there's more to learn. My continued searches for information led me to J.D. Lenzen's work, specifically his *Tying It All Together* (TIAT) YouTube channel.

J.D.'s video instructions are straightforward and easy to understand. For him, cord is a fluid medium. He takes simple, fundamental knot elements and recombines them to create new knots and ties. A method of tying that has come to be known as fusion knotting. With each technique he teaches, he encourages and inspires others to take what they've learned and in his words, "Explore, Discover, Innovate!".

When it comes to this book, it doesn't matter if you're a knot novice or an expert with years of functional tying experience. People from all walks of life can take a length of cord and duplicate J.D.'s ties. He starts with familiar (historical) ties, like the Diamond Knot, Solomon Bar, and Monkey's Fist, and builds upon these to create fusion ties incorporating slip knots, hitches, and crossed cords. His talent as a photographer and writer enables him to provide readers with clear and concise instructions. And his use of bright and visually contrasting colors helps readers follow the path of each cord, through each step of a tie, from beginning to end.

I've re-created many of J.D.'s fusion knots and ties, my favorites being patterns used to make paracord bracelets and watchbands. But I know I've really only scratched the surface. I look forward to tying more and finding different ways to utilize his techniques, and I'm motivated to keep learning as the new ideas just keep coming!

David Hopper (Stormdrane)
stormdrane.blogspot.com
April 2012

Acknowledgments

For their support and/or inspiration in the production of this book, I would like to thank Clifford W. Ashley, my parents (Jim and Barbara), the subscribers to my *Tying It All Together* YouTube channel, and the members of the fusion knotting community as a whole. Without you, especially those who continue to support my online videos, this book would not have come to be.

And…

A very special thanks to my wife and my muse, Kristen Kakos. Your presence in my life brings me joy, comfort, and the freedom to create. For these gifts I am forever grateful.

Introduction

Clifford W. Ashley, the famed author of *The Ashley Book of Knots* (ABOK)—a book widely considered to be the "Bible" of knot tying—invented new knots…and there were many. From stopper knots to bends to innovative expansions of a multitude of decorative knots, Ashley utilized his vast knowledge to reconfigure what was known, integrate unique twists and turns, and create knots anew. But something strange happened on the way to the bookstore. Since its initial publication in the summer of 1944, ABOK has inspired a dogmatic reverence for historical knots more than the creation of new and innovative ones, despite Ashley's clearly expressed approval of the latter.

Evidence of this restrained vision was no more apparent than during the fanfare that surrounded Dr. Edward Hunter's 1978 "discovery" of the Hunter's Bend. A means the doctor used to tie his broken shoelaces, the bend was a front page story in the London Times. And why not? New knots, the belief was, weren't created every day. And the eventual realization that the bend had already been discovered 35 years earlier by Phil D. Smith, only served to reinforce this belief.

Then came the Internet, or more specifically an opportunity for knot tyers and knot enthusiasts from all around the world to join together as a single community. A community not only interested in historical knots and ties, but newly discovered ones as well.

It was about this time that I was quietly developing the tying techniques that would come to be known as fusion knotting—the creation of innovative knots and ties through the merging of different knot elements or knotting techniques. The year was 1995, and I was living in Loma Mar, California, working as a naturalist at an outdoor education school called Exploring New Horizons.

Loma Mar is a very small town and I had no Internet access while I lived there. I also didn't have a television or a stable radio station to listen to, so I spent most of my nights and weekends studying historical knots, breaking them down into their component parts and reconfiguring them into new knots and ties. With few social connections or much of a social life, I logged my discoveries in a notebook and (for the most part) kept my findings to myself.

A year later, I started graduate school. Swept up into the demands of my research and academic studies, I didn't do much tying. But upon my graduation in 1999 I had more time on my hands and so started tying again.

My three year break from tying did me good. With my life now a predictable routine, I found myself experiencing an unprecedented flow of new ideas and techniques. No longer content with logging my discoveries in a notebook, I began teaching my fusion knotting methods to others. Through teaching, I learned what others needed to see, feel, and hear, to understand. Although the connections I made during this period of my life were massively rewarding, my reach felt limited. I wanted to spread my fusion knotting techniques around the

Introduction

world, connect with a broader spectrum of people, and shatter the paradigm that knotting was a finite field of study; and I needed a method beyond my presence in a room to make that happen.

That method arrived in early 2007, when my then girlfriend (now wife), Kristen, gave me a digital camera for my 35th birthday. It was a PowerShot SD800 IS and its video function allowed me to create movies. Realizing that videos would be the means for me to connect with and contribute to the larger worldwide knot tying community, I joined YouTube and registered the video channel name *Tying It All Together* (TIAT).

On September 7, 2008, I released my first TIAT instructional video, a historical tie, "How to Make a Military Bugle Cord". My teaching style and pace were well received and I continued making instructional videos, once a week, for nearly three years straight (semiweekly during late 2011).

Since 2008, I've produced over 200 instructional videos, cultivated a subscriber base of over 60,000 people (as of the date of this publication), launched FusionKnots.com, established the Fusion Knots Forum (an online forum dedicated to exchanging information and insights regarding fusion knots and ties), and produced my first knot instruction book, *Decorative Fusion Knots: A Step-by-Step Illustrated Guide to New and Unusual Ornamental Knots* (2011).

In *Decorative Fusion Knots* (DFK) I touched upon a tying material I'd been familiar with for years, but hadn't spent much

time using. That material was paracord—the reason why you're holding this book.

My current day job involves occasional work on military bases, where I'm routinely exposed to paracord—a lightweight nylon kernmantle cord originally used as parachute suspension lines during World War II. Spools of it lay around active base workshops, maintenance yards, and other places a strong, lightweight cord might be needed.

I'd long admired paracord for its versatility and usefulness, and recognized there was a community of tyers who used it exclusively to create their pieces. But the colors I initially saw it come in were limited—foliage green, coyote brown, and black. These colors led me to believe paracord only existed in hues that wouldn't contrast well in my TIAT videos. Shortly thereafter, I discovered paracord came in a wide variety of colors. So I purchased a couple of hanks and gave my fusion knotting techniques a go.

The results of my explorations with paracord have been fantastically fruitful, as evident by the numerical abundance of new fusion knots and ties I've discovered through its use. Given the volume of paracord ties I've produced over the years (created privately and presented publically through TIAT) I decided it was time to generate a literary repository of my paracord works. This book is volume one of that effort.

Play with, practice, and explore the paracord fusion ties within this book. But do so knowing these ties and techniques

Introduction

are merely springboards for what can and will be. As Ashley demonstrated in his seminal book and I'll restate here, knotting is not a finite field of study. The only thing keeping you and the rest of the world from experiencing and learning new knots and ties is creative desire. Don't fall prey to the belief that what you see is all that can be. The future is limitless, and that limitless future is now!

JD of *Tying It All Together*

About Paracord

Background

Paracord is a lightweight nylon rope constructed with a core of yarns wrapped in a woven exterior sheath. The yarns of paracord establish the maximum stress the rope can withstand while being stretched or pulled, and the exterior sheath protects the yarns from abrasion. The word *paracord* derives from its original use as suspension lines for U.S. parachutes during World War II. This said, on account of paracord's utility, paratroopers used it for a variety of other tasks once on the ground.

As with other materials and technologies originally slated for military use, paracord has since become a widely valued rope in civilian circles. Its commercial availability (not surprisingly) was initially pressed forward by military veterans who'd grown accustomed to its use during service. Over the years support for its availability has been equally heralded by gun and knife collectors, hunters, survivalists, do-it-yourself (DIY) makers, as well as an ever-growing community of paracord crafters.

Types

The U.S. military describes six types of paracord (Type I, IA, II, IIA, III, and IV). However, for the purposes of the information provided in this book and the fundamental "need to know" knowledge of the readers, paracord is generally available in two forms, Type II and III. Type II paracord is conventionally called 450 paracord (minimum strength 450 pounds) and usually has a core consisting of 4 two-ply yarns. Type III paracord is referred to as 550 paracord (minimum strength 550 pounds) and typically has a core consisting of 7 two-ply yarns.

The ties presented in this book were

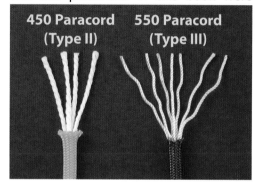

created with 450 paracord. I used 450 paracord because I enjoy its pliability (it's very amenable to fusion knotting techniques) and the variety of colors it comes in. However, 550 paracord and a wide variety of other cord types, including (but not limited to) solid braid nylon, hemp, satin, fabric, leather cords, and even wire, could be used to create all the designs shown in this book. In short, if in doubt, give it a tie!

Sources

If living in the U.S., your paracord purchasing options are many, and include army surplus stores, hardware stores, and (in some communities) arts and craft stores. Be this as it may, not all people reading this book live in the U.S. or have access to (local) storefront paracord vendors. If this is you, don't worry. Thankfully, there are online vendors who sell paracord, and they ship both domestically and internationally.

About Paracord

The following is a list of online paracord vendors. My hope is that one of them will meet your paracord needs.

armynavystoreinc.com	paracord.com	supplycaptain.com
atwoodrope.net	paracord.no	survival-pax.com
bucklerunner.com	paracordcity.com	takknife.com
campingsurvival.com	paracordplanet.com	the550cordshop.com
cheaperthandirt.com	paracordstore.com	thebushcraftstore.co.uk
coolglowstuff.com	redflarekits.com	theparacordstore.co.uk
delksarmynavysurplus.com	rwrope.com	topbrassmilitary.com
fullbellyinsurance.com	shoprobbys.com	touwhandel.nl
gorillaparacord.com	sosakonline.com	ubraidit.com
greatadventure.ca	stores.ebay.com/AnS-Tactical	vtarmynavy.com
onestopknifeshop.com	stores.ebay.com/Five-Star-EDC	whitemoosetradingco.com
parachute-cord.com	stores.ebay.com/ParaClocks	wholesale-parachute-cord.com

Note: Because of the dynamic nature of the Internet, any web addresses or links contained in this book may have changed since publication and may no longer be valid. Further, any and all vendor information provided does not constitute an endorsement or recommendation by the publisher or the author.

About This Book

Instruction Format

The intent of this book is to provide all the information necessary to successfully complete each knot or tie presented while minimizing redundant procedures. In turn, procedures performed on every knot or tie, such as snipping and singeing, are shown only once (see next page) and then simply referenced as a procedure to be performed in the instruction text (i.e., "Carefully snip and singe the ends."). In those cases when a finishing knot is routinely used, such as the 2-Strand Diamond Knot and the 4-Strand Diamond Knot, the instruction text calls out the knot to be tied accompanied by the page number where that knot was first shown. These "notable knots," as well as others, are detailed further in the next section.

Notable Knots

The following four knots are incorporated into multiple ties within this book:

- **2-Strand Diamond Knot** (Page 2)
- **4-Strand Diamond Knot** (Page 5)
- **Triangle Tie Off** (Page 60)
- **Stopper Knot** (Page 112)

The 2-Strand Diamond Knot and the Stopper Knot are used to assist in the clasping of bracelets. The 4-Strand Diamond Knot and the Triangle Tie Off are used to fix or lock a tie in place. Aside from allowing the clean finishing of a tie, these last two knots may also be used as transition knots for setting up the ability to tie a clasp knot (i.e., the 2-Strand Diamond Knot).

Note: Diamond knots can be tied clockwise or counterclockwise. However, for instructability the 2-Strand Diamond Knot is shown tied in its counterclockwise orientation, and the 4-Strand Diamond Knot is shown tied in its clockwise orientation.

Special Sizing

I'm often asked how much paracord one needs to make a specific length of a given tie (e.g. "How much cord do I need to make a 30 inch long Blaze Bar belt?"). Questions like these aren't as easy to answer as they first appear, on account of the following:

A) Paracord (purchased from varying sources) has varying degrees of elasticity and thickness;

B) Each tyer has his or her own degree of tightening; and

C) Different phases of a tie utilize different lengths of cord (i.e., the beginning of a tie uses up one amount of cord per inch, and the middle of a tie uses a different amount, as does the end of a tie).

On top of that, if someone leans on one of my ballpark estimates, purchases cord, cuts it to length, and attempts their desired tie, only to find they're short inches or more of their goal, I become the "bad guy" for misinforming them. So I tend not to answer such questions directly, and instead encourage people to work out special sizing requirements on their own.

All that said, in consideration of the

About This Book

information just provided, a tyer can generally determine how much paracord they'll need to make a specific length of tie by tying an inch of that tie, then untying it, and seeing how much cord was used. The ratio revealed becomes a means of estimating how much total paracord will be required (e.g. if 2 feet of cord is used to make 1 inch of bar, then 6 feet of cord will be required to make a 3 inch bar).

Snipping & Singeing

Paracord is made of nylon, and nylon is a thermoplastic (also known as a thermosoftening plastic). Put another way, nylon is a polymer that turns into a liquid when heated. During this heated state it can be molded. When it comes to paracord ties this molding flares the "glassed" ends of the cord, making them larger than the cinched loop holding them in place.

For the most part, this change in physical state seals paracord ends until a greater (human sourced) force is applied (i.e. the flared ends are pulled through the cinched loop and/or the fused glassed ends are broken).

The following section presents the step-by-step procedure used to snip and singe the ends of all the paracord ties shown in this book.

How to Snip & Singe Cord Ends

1. Begin with the possession of the following items: **Barber Shears** and a **Butane Torch Lighter**

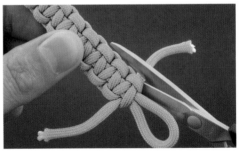

2. Once the desired tie length is achieved, carefully snip the undesired cord ends off with your shears.

3. Once the undesired cord ends are removed…

4. …ready your lighter. Make sure to keep hands away from the lighter tip.

About This Book

5. Quickly (no more than 1 to 2 seconds) singe the first snipped end of your cord…

6. …and then the second. While the "glassed" ends of your snipped paracord are still soft…

7. …but no longer hot to the touch, mold them with your thumb.

8. Congratulations, you've successfully sealed the ends of your paracord tie in place!

WARNING: Children should not use shears (i.e., scissors) or lighters without adult supervision. If you're reading this, and you're not sure if this warning applies to you…it probably does. Stop, show these instructions to a competent parent or guardian, and ask for their assistance.

Twists & Terms

The following definitions and visual clarifications are meant to provide an understanding of the knotting procedures and terms associated with this book.

Definitions

ABOK: Acronym for *The Ashley Book of Knots*.

Bar: A semi-ridged, tightly constructed, tie typically made with square knots (e.g. Solomon Bar).

Bight: A line doubled over into a U-shape.

Circle: A line making one complete revolution around another line or body part (e.g. a finger).

Clockwise Loop: A loop that has a running end (or line on top) that rotates clockwise.

Coil: A line that makes several (more than one) revolutions around another line or body part (e.g. a finger).

Component Part: A knot element or knotting technique used to make a fusion knot or tie.

Cord: A slender length of flexible material used to make a knot or tie.

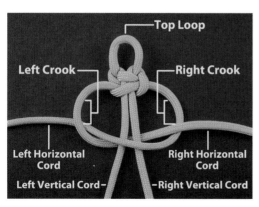

Cord Parts

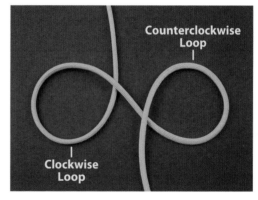

Cord Loops

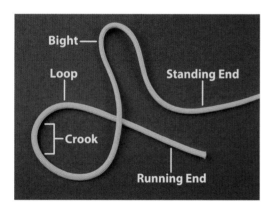

Tie Parts

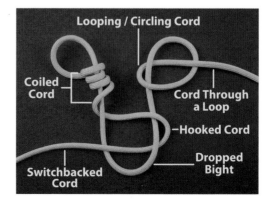

Tie Movements

Twists & Terms

Counterclockwise Loop: A loop that has a running end (or line on top) that rotates counterclockwise.

Crook: The curved inside part of a bight, circle, loop, or hooked line.

DFK: Acronym for the book *Decorative Fusion Knots.*

Fall: Shorthand for the genre of ties known as Endless Falls.

Firm: The point at which the adjusting of a knot results in a satisfactory appearance.

Firmly Tightening: Tightening until the knot or tie is as taut as one can make it.

Flip: Turning a knot, tie, or semi-completed knot or tie over, upside down, vertically, or horizontally.

Fusion Tie: An innovative tie created through the merging of different knot elements or knotting techniques.

Historical Knot: A knot (or tie) that was discovered or created before 1979 (the year the IGKT updated ABOK).

Hook: A line that makes a sharp curve or shape resembling a hook, typically around a line.

Horizontal: Referring to a flat or level position.

IGKT: Acronym for the International Guild of Knot Tyers.

Key Fob: A generally decorative, at times useful, item or tie that connects to a key ring or key.

Lace: A threaded cord used to tie opposite ends together.

Legs: Dangling or vertical parallel cords.

Lightly Tightening: Tightening until the knot or tie sufficiently maintains a design, spacing, or a latticed appearance.

Line: The material used to tie a knot or tie (e.g. paracord, rope, wire, etc.).

Loop: A circle of line that crosses itself or a bight cinched at its base.

P: A line that is looped to look like the letter P or the mirror image of the letter P.

Paracord: A lightweight nylon rope constructed with a core of yarns wrapped in a woven exterior sheath.

Parallel: Two straight lines or cords maintaining an equal distance from one another.

Piece: The partially completed or final version of an entire knot or tie.

Running End: The end of a line that is being used to make the knot or tie.

Singe: Scorching the end of a cut line to hold it in place or keep it from fraying.

Sinnet: A weaving technique or tie generally performed with a series of slip knots, used to shorten the length of a line.

Twists & Terms

Standing End: The end of a line that is not involved in making the knot or tie.

TIAT: Acronym for the YouTube video channel *Tying It All Together*.

Tuck: Inserting a line or bight through a loop or under another line.

Vertical: Referring to an upright position, at a right angle to the horizon.

Viceroy Tie: A tie that mimics the appearance, but not the actual tying technique, of a historical tie.

Weave: Passing a line over and under another line.

Chapter 1

Diamonds,
Balls, & Bundles

2-STRAND DIAMOND KNOT

A few steps beyond a Carrick Bend (shown below), the 2-Strand Diamond Knot is a quick way to add a decorative cylindrical weave to an otherwise dull cord. The knot is also the clasp that will be used for most of the paracord bracelets shown in this book.

Cord Used: *Two 5 In. Cord Ends (Minimum Length)*

Component Parts: *Historical Knot*

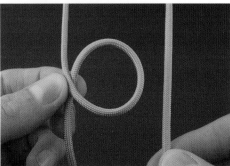

1. Make a clockwise **P** with the left cord.

2. Lift the right running end up, behind the loop of the **P**.

3. Drop the running end down, over the cord above the **P**, and under the "leg" of the **P**.

4. Bight the running end and weave it over, under, and over the cords to the right.

5. Pull the bight out to form a Carrick Bend.

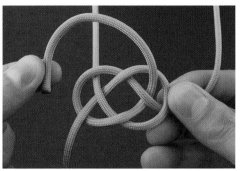

6. Now, hook the right running end left, over the (left) cord above the Carrick Bend…

7. ...and insert it through the (back) center of the Carrick Bend.

8. Then, hook the left running end right, over the (right) cord above the Carrick Bend...

9. ...and insert it through the (back) center of the Carrick Bend.

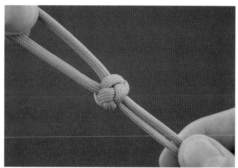

10. Adjust the cord ends until the 2-Strand Diamond Knot is firm and symmetrical.

DIAMOND WATERFALL

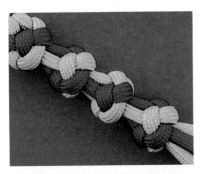

The Diamond Waterfall is a line of strategically placed 4-Strand Diamond Knots. The fob version of the tie (shown below) dangles off my personal ring of keys. Sliding nicely between fingers and knuckles, the tie is easy to grip and handle.

Cord Used: *Two 3 Ft. Cords (3 In. Key Fob)*

Component Parts: *Diamond Knot + Series + Integrated Contrasting Cords + 3/4 In. Split Ring*

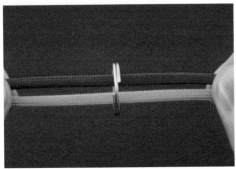

1. Lace the two cords through a split ring until their middles are reached.

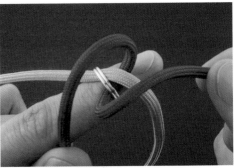

2. Arch one of the cords over the other, twice, in opposite directions.

3. Weave one end of the straight cord over its first arch…

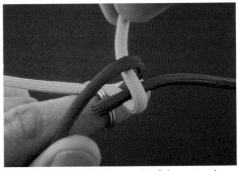

4. …and through the crook of the second arch.

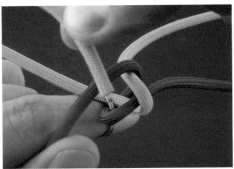

5. Weave the other end of the straight cord over its first arch…

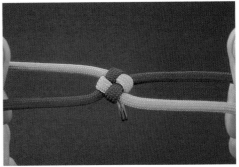

6. …and through the crook of the second arch. Tighten to form a Crown Knot.

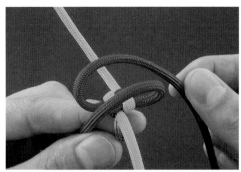

7. **4-Strand Diamond Knot:** Arch two cord ends, from the same cord, in opposite directions.

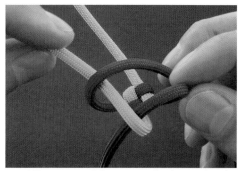

8. Weave one of the perpendicular cord ends over its first arch and through the crook of the second arch.

9. Weave the other perpendicular cord end over its first arch and through the crook of the second arch.

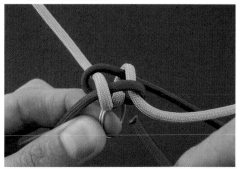

10. Now, hook the right cord end clockwise, around the arched cord beside it…

11. …and insert it through the center of the Crown Knot.

12. Hook the next cord end (below the one before) clockwise, around the arched cord beside it…

13. …and insert it through the center of the Crown Knot.

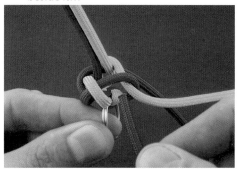

14. Hook the next cord end (below the one before) clockwise, around the arched cord beside it…

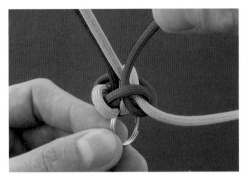

15. …and insert it through the center of the Crown Knot.

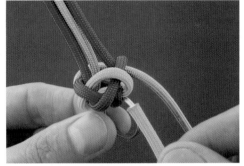

16. Finally, hook the last cord end clockwise, around the arched cord beside it…

17. …and insert it through the center of the Crown Knot.

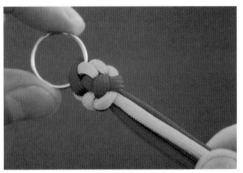

18. Adjust the cords until the 4-Strand Diamond Knot is firm and symmetrical.

19. A "thumb pinch" distance after the first knot repeat Steps 7 through 18.

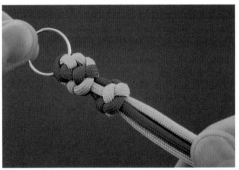

20. Again, adjust the cords until the knot is firm and symmetrical.

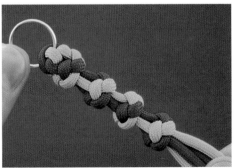

21. Tie 3 to 4 diamond knots, a thumb pinch apart from one another.

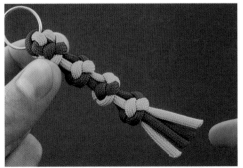

22. Once desired fob length is achieved, carefully snip and singe the ends.

MONKEY'S FIST (TWO COLOR)

The Monkey's Fist is a classic knot historically used to add weight or grip to the end of a tossed line. More recently, the knot has become a favored piece among paracord tyers attracted to its clean round shape.

Cord Used: *Two 2.5 Ft. Cords (1.0 In. Dia. Ball)*

Component Parts: *Monkey's Fist + Integrated Contrasting Cords*

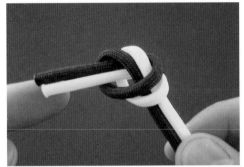

1. Start by tying the tips of the two cords together with an Overhand Knot.

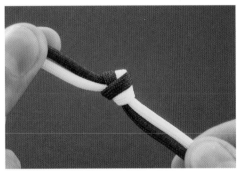

2. Tighten the knot until firm.

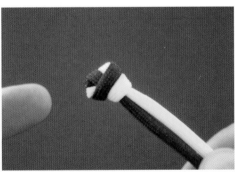

3. Once done tightening, carefully snip off the cord ends above the knot.

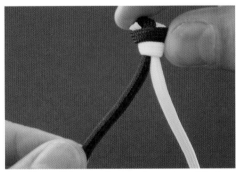

4. Now, slide your fingers down one of the cords…

5. …approximately 15 inches. At this point…

6. …start circling the cord around two split fingers. Circling once…

7.   …twice…

8.   …and a third time, or until the Overhand Knot is halfway between the coiled cords.

9.   Insert the Overhand Knot into the center of the vertical coils.

10.   Then start circling the running end (beyond the knot) away from you and around the vertical coils.

11.   Circling once, twice…

12.   …and a third time, stacking each circle on top of the other, creating a second set of coils.

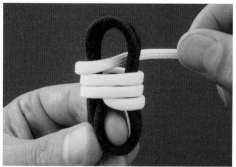

13.   Slide the tie off your fingers. Then start circling the running end away from you…

14.   …and around the horizontal coils…

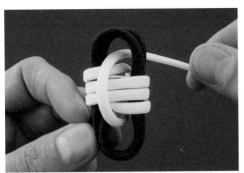

15. …making sure to start circling…

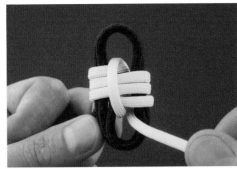

16. …from left…

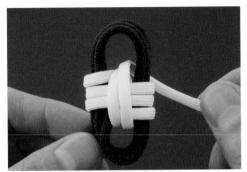

17. …to right…

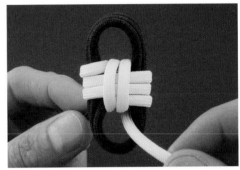

18. …until…

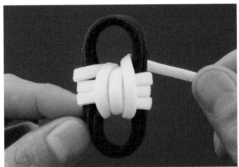

19. …three circles, vertical to the horizontal coils, have been made.

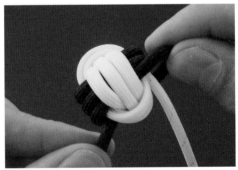

20. Adjust the cords until the piece is firm,

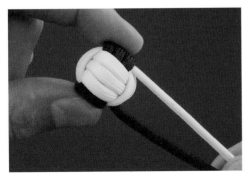

21. …or until all three sets of coils are snugly wrapped around the Overhand Knot.

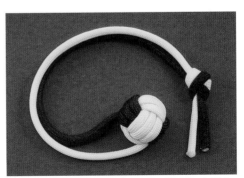

22. Carefully snip and singe the Monkey's Fist ends for a stand alone piece, or leave a tether.

PARACORD BALLS

Paracord Balls are more often seen, than clearly understood. Glancing eyes dismiss them as Monkey's Fists. But, more factually, they are rounded 3-lead 4-bight Turk's Heads. Relatively easy to tie, the balls make really cool gifts.

Cord Used: *4 Ft. Cord (0.5 In. Dia. Ball)*

Component Parts: *Historical Knot*

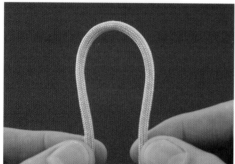

1. Eight inches right of the left cord end, make a bight.

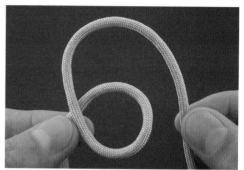

2. Then make a clockwise **P** with the left (descending) cord.

3. Drop the right running end down in front of the loop of the **P**.

4. Bight the running end. Then weave it under the "leg" of the **P**…

5. …over the cord above it, under the top of the **P**, over itself, and under…

6. …the right bottom of the **P**. Pull the bight out to form a Double Coin Knot.

7. Now, weave the right running end over the lower left loop of the Double Coin Knot…

8. …and alongside (parallel to) the crook of the left standing end.

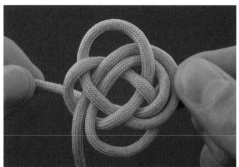

9. Keep weaving the running end alongside the crook…

10. …passing it under and over the cords before it…

11. …until…

12. …the running end…

13. …reaches…

14. …the crook of the point where it started. This is (effectively) a 3-lead 4-bight Turk's Head.

15. Insert the running end through the crook of the lower left loop.

16. Flip the piece over, vertically, and tie an Overhand Knot…

17. …firmly against the base of the Turk's Head.

18. Carefully snip off the cord ends beyond the knot.

19. Flip the piece back over, vertically.

20. Collapse the Turk's Head around the Overhand Knot on the opposite side.

21. Continue shaping, pulling up slack, and adjusting the cords until a tight ball forms.

22. Once desired firmness is achieved, carefully snip and singe the Paracord Ball end.

TINY GLOBE KNOT

The Tiny Globe Knot is an innovative way of tying a standard Globe Knot. Making use of a forefinger for knotting support, the following instructions illustrate how this historically complex knot can be tied in hand.

Cord Used: *One 4 Ft. Cord (1 In. Dia. Ball)*

Component Parts: *Globe Knot + Innovative Technique + 0.5 In. Dia. Marble*

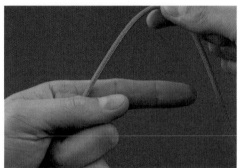

1. Start at the middle of the cord. Grip one end and extend the other end up.

2. Circle the cord around your forefinger once…

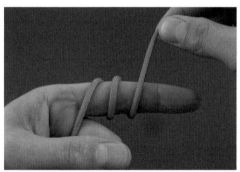

3. …twice…

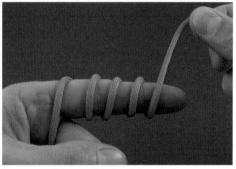

4. …and then a third and fourth time.

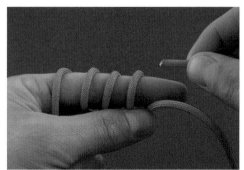

5. With the tip of the right running end in hand…

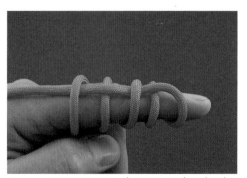

6. …weave it over, under, over, and under the vertical cords to the left.

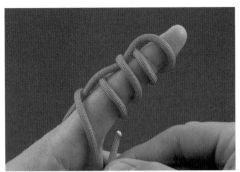

7. Then, with the tip of the left running end in hand…

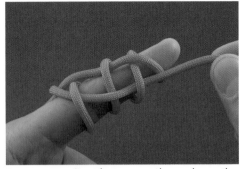

8. …weave it under, over, under, and over the vertical cords to the right.

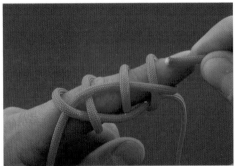

9. Hook the same running end up and left…

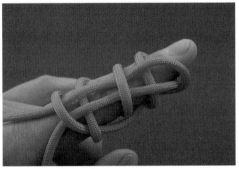

10. …and weave it alongside the outside of the top horizontal cord.

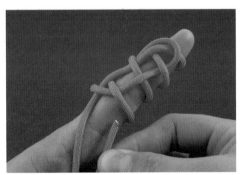

11. Hook the other running end down and right…

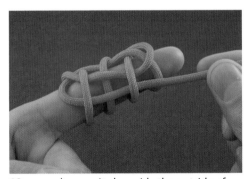

12. …and weave it alongside the outside of the bottom horizontal cord.

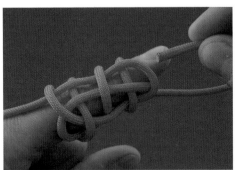

13. With the top two horizontal cords separated, hook the same running end up and left.

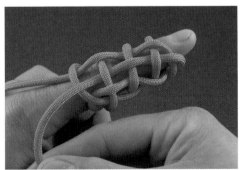

14. Then weave it over, under, over, under, and over the vertical cords between.

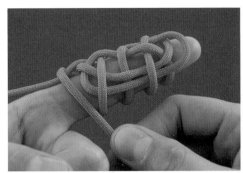

15. Drop the other running end down over the cord beneath it.

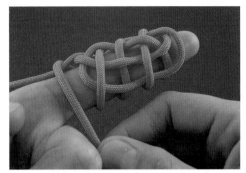

16. With the bottom two horizontal cords separated, hook the same running end right.

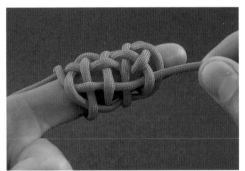

17. Then weave it under, over, under, over, and under the vertical cords between.

18. Slide the piece off your finger and rotate it a quarter turn, vertically (i.e. spin the piece 45°, away from you).

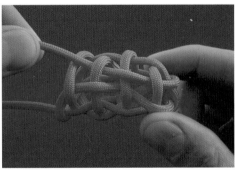

19. Weave the right running end over, under, over, under and over the vertical cords between the horizontal (parallel) cords.

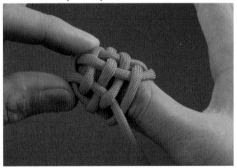

20. Shape the "basket" made with your thumb.

21. Take hold of a 0.5 inch diameter marble…

22. …and insert it into the center of the basket.

23. Shape and pull up slack until a tight symmetrical wrap forms around the marble.

24. Carefully snip and singe the Tiny Globe Knot ends for a stand alone piece, or leave a tether.

Chapter 2

Wisdom
of Solomon

ELASTIC SOLOMON BAR

The Elastic Solomon Bar is a quick way to make a one-size-fits-all bracelet, as a gift for others or yourself. Surprisingly simple to make, the bracelet is the product of a standard Solomon Bar wrapped around a metal-free elastic band (or hair tie).

Cord Used: *One 6 Ft. Cord (Varying Sized Bracelet)*

Component Parts: *Solomon Bar + Elastic Band*

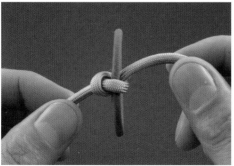

1. Start with an elastic band in hand.

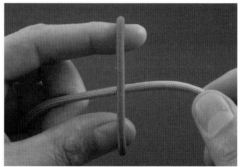

2. Lace the cord through the elastic band until its middle is reached.

3. Hook the right running end left, over the elastic band.

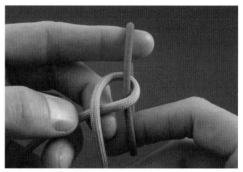

4. Drop the left running end over the cord beneath it.

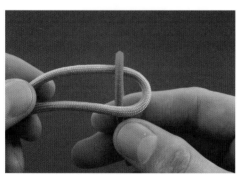

5. Then hook it right, under the elastic band, and through the back of the right crook. Tighten lightly.

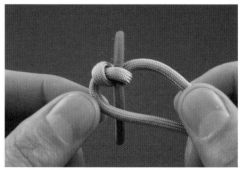

6. Hook the left running end left, over the elastic band.

7. Drop the right running end over the cord beneath it.

8. Then hook it left, under the elastic band, and through the back of the left crook. Tighten lightly.

9. Repeat Steps 3 through 8 until the elastic band is circled. Tighten the last knot firmly.

10. Carefully snip and singe the Solomon Bar ends for a one-size-fits-all bracelet!

SOLOMON BAR (TWO COLOR)

The Solomon Bar is the foundation piece for paracord tyers. Clean looking and relatively easy to generate, the tie's engineering elegance is only matched by its versatility. The following shows how to make a two color version of the bar.

Cord Used: *Two 4 Ft. Cords (7.5 In. Bracelet)*

Component Parts: *Solomon Bar + Integrated Contrasting Cords*

1. Draw the two cords out side-by-side the length of the desired bracelet, plus (+) 5 inches.

2. With the short cord ends facing down, grip your measured point.

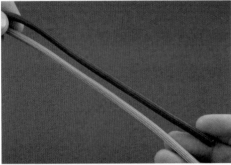

3. Hook the right running end left, over the vertical cords.

4. Drop the left running end over the cord beneath it.

5. Then hook it right and through the back of the right loop.

6. Insert the tip of the right running end through the front of the left loop.

7. Insert the tip of the left running end through the back of the right loop.

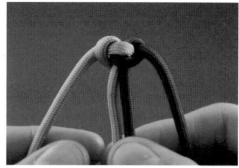

8. Tighten the piece until firm.

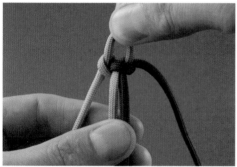

9. Pull the top cord up to make a 0.5 inch bight.

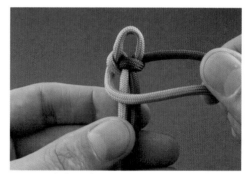

10. Hook the left running end right, over the vertical cords.

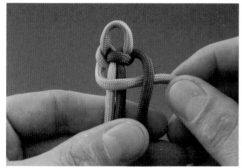

11. Drop the right running end over the cord beneath it.

12. Then hook it left, under the vertical cords, and through the back of the left crook. Tighten firmly.

13. Hook the right running end left, over the vertical cords.

14. Drop the left running end over the cord beneath it.

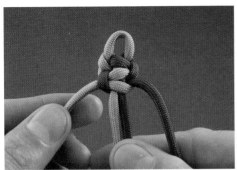

15. Then hook it right, under the vertical cords, and through the back of the right crook. Tighten firmly.

16. Repeat Steps 10 through 15 until a minimum 5 inches of cord ends remain.

17. Carefully snip and singe the horizontal cord ends.

18. Tie a 2-Strand Diamond Knot (See Page 2) with the vertical cords.

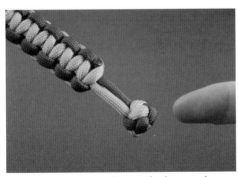

19. Carefully snip and singe the knot ends.

20. The completed Solomon Bar Bracelet— back side out.

STITCHED SOLOMON BAR

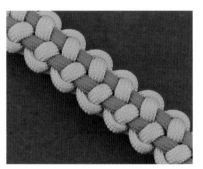

The Stitched Solomon Bar generates double stitched lines on an otherwise standard bar. The bracelet version of the tie (shown below) is super easy to fit to your wrist. Just keep tying until the length you need is reached.

Cord Used: *One 6 Ft. & 3 Ft. Cord (7.5 In. Bracelet)*

Component Parts: *Solomon Bar + Split Weave + Contrasting Cords*

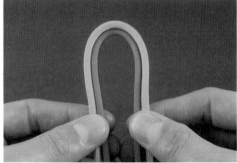

1. Start with bights created at the middle of the two cords.

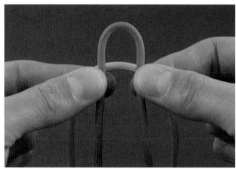

2. Drop the long cord down 0.5 inch, behind the bight of the short cord.

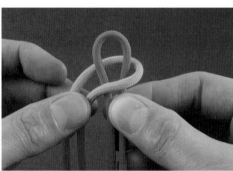

3. Hook the right running end left, over the vertical cords.

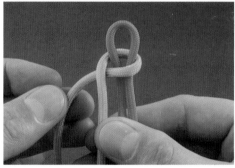

4. Drop the left running end over the cord beneath it.

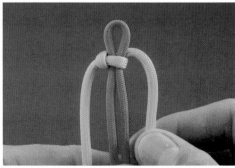

5. Then hook it right, under the vertical cords, and through the back of the right crook. Tighten firmly.

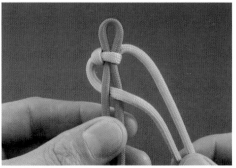

6. Weave the left running end right, under, and over the vertical cords.

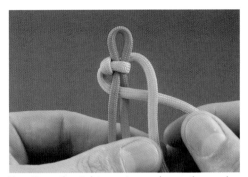

7. Drop the right running end over the cord beneath it.

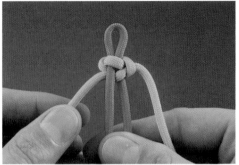

8. Then hook it left, under the vertical cords, and through the back of the left crook. Tighten firmly.

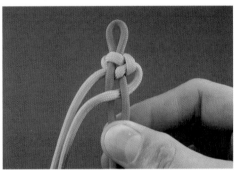

9. Weave the right running end left, under, and over the vertical cords.

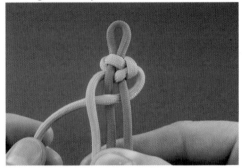

10. Drop the left running end over the cord beneath it.

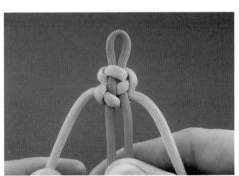

11. Then hook it right, under the vertical cords, and through the back of the right crook. Tighten firmly.

12. Repeat Steps 6 through 11 until a minimum 5 inches of cord ends remain.

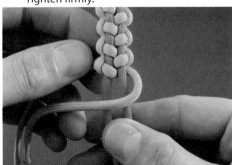

13. Now, hook the right running end left, over the vertical cords.

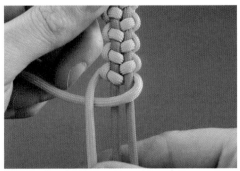

14. Drop the left running end over the cord beneath it.

15. Then hook it right, under the vertical cords, and through the back of the right crook. Tighten firmly.

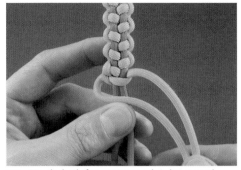

16. Hook the left running end right, over the vertical cords.

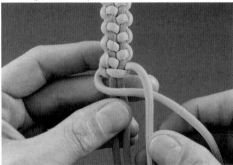

17. Drop the right running end over the cord beneath it.

18. Then hook it left, under the vertical cords, and through the back of the left crook. Tighten firmly.

19. Carefully snip and singe the horizontal cord ends.

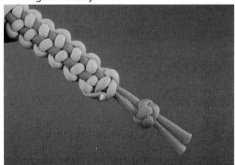

20. Tie a 2-Strand Diamond Knot (See Page 2) with the vertical cords.

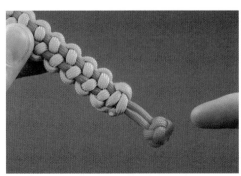

21. Carefully snip and singe the knot ends.

22. The completed Stitched Solomon Bar Bracelet—front side out.

CRISSCROSSED SOLOMON BAR

The Crisscrossed Solomon Bar is a flourish that turns a classic Solomon Bar into something extra special. Great looking as a bracelet, the tie can be worn right-side up or right-side down, because both sides have a unique appearance.

Cord Used: *One 6 Ft. & 4 Ft. Cord (7.5 In. Bracelet)*

Component Parts: *Solomon Bar + Crossed Cords + Contrasting Cords*

1. With the long cord, draw out a bight the length of the desired bracelet.

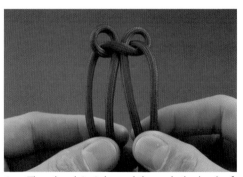

2. Hook the right running end left, over the vertical cords.

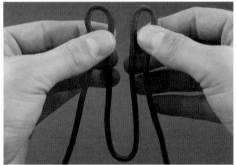

3. Drop the left running end over the cord beneath it.

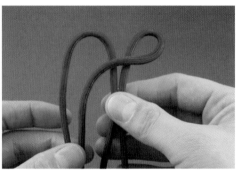

4. Then hook it right and through the back of the right loop.

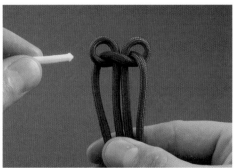

5. Take the tip of the short cord in hand…

6. …and lace it through the back of the left loop…

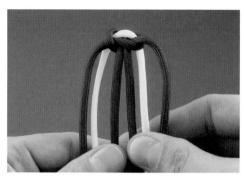

7. …then the front of the right loop. Stop lacing when the middle of the cord is reached.

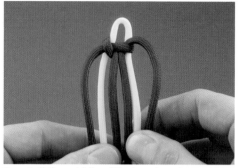

8. Pull the middle of the laced cord up to make a 0.5 inch bight. Tighten in place firmly.

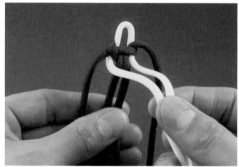

9. Now, pull the laced cords forward.

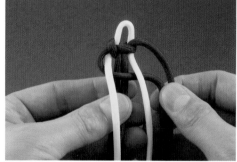

10. Hook the left running end right, over the vertical cords and under the laced cords.

11. Drop the right running end over the cord beneath it.

12. Then hook it left, under the vertical cords, and through the back of the left crook. Tighten firmly.

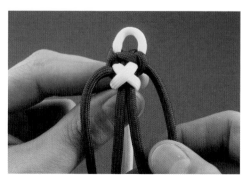

13. Cross the laced cords over the vertical cords, right over left.

14. Hook the right running end left, over the vertical cords and the laced cords.

15. Drop the left running end over the cord beneath it.

16. Then hook it right, under the vertical cords, and through the back of the right crook. Tighten firmly.

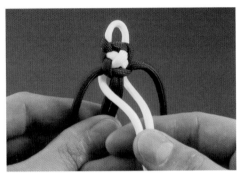

17. Pull the laced cords forward.

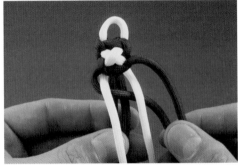

18. Hook the left running end right, over the vertical cords and under the laced cords.

19. Drop the right running end over the cord beneath it.

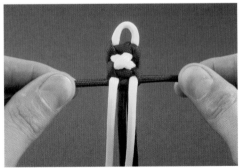

20. Then hook it right, under the vertical cords, and through the back of the right crook. Tighten firmly.

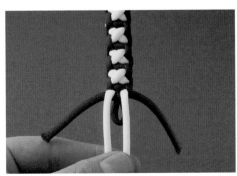

21. Repeat Steps 13 through 20 until 0.5 inch short of desired length.

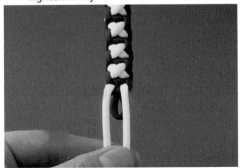

22. Carefully snip and singe the horizontal cord ends.

23. Take the tips of the laced cords in hand,...

24. ...and insert them through the bight at the bottom of the piece.

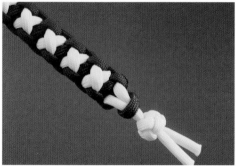

25. Now, tie a 2-Strand Diamond Knot (See Page 2) with the vertical (laced) cords.

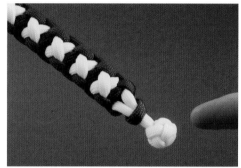

26. Carefully snip and singe the knot ends.

27. Both sides of the Crisscrossed Solomon Bar Bracelet look different...

28. ...so you actually have two bracelets in one!

DOUBLE-SOLOMON BAR (THIN LINE)

"Thin Line" Double Solomon Bars are often made as gifts for those who risk their lives in the service of others. This tie is especially significant to me, because my father (now retired) served as a police officer in Oakland, California, for 21 years.

Cord Used: *One 8 Ft. & 1.5 Ft. Cord (3.5 In. Key Fob)*

Component Parts: *Solomon Bar + Solomon Bar + Contrasting Line of Cord*

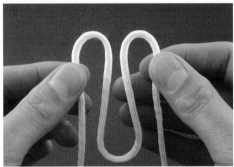

1. With the long cord, draw out a bight the length of the desired fob plus (+) 1 inch.

2. Hook the right running end left, over the vertical cords.

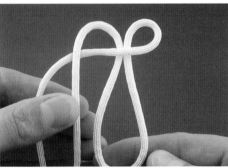

3. Drop the left running end over the cord beneath it.

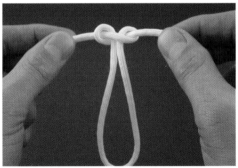

4. Then hook it right and through the back of the right loop. Tighten firmly.

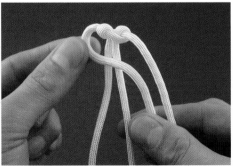

5. Hook the left running end right, over the vertical cords.

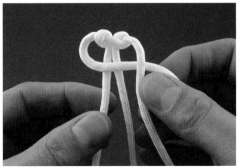

6. Drop the right running end over the cord beneath it.

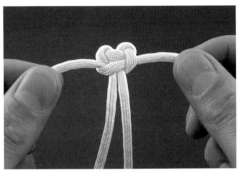

7. Then hook it left, under the vertical cords, and through the back of the left crook. Tighten lightly.

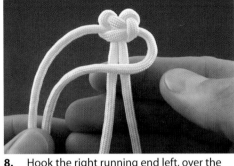

8. Hook the right running end left, over the vertical cords.

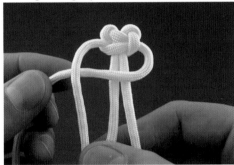

9. Drop the left running end over the cord beneath it.

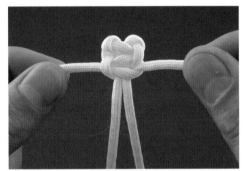

10. Then hook it right, under the vertical cords, and through the back of the right crook. Tighten firmly.

11. Repeat Steps 5 through 10 until a 1 inch loop remains.

12. Flip the piece over, vertically.

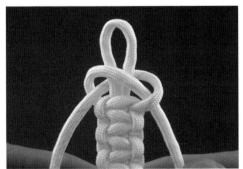

13. Loosen the top tie.

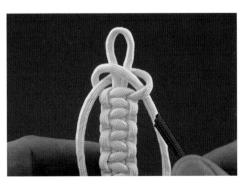

14. Then take the tip of the short cord in hand…

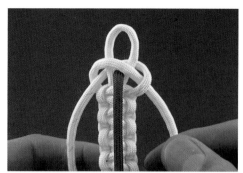

15. …and lace it through the top loop, beneath the loosened tie.

16. Once the middle of the laced cord is reached, tighten the top tie firmly.

17. Hook the right running end left, over the laced cord.

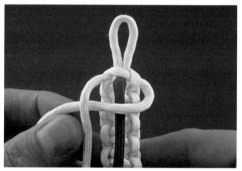

18. Drop the left running end over the cord beneath it.

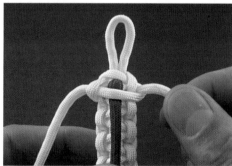

19. Then hook it right, over the laced cord (in back), and through the back of the right crook. Tighten firmly.

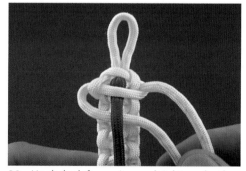

20. Hook the left running end right, under the laced cord.

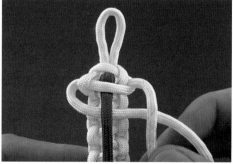

21. Drop the right running end over the cord beneath it. Then hook it left…

22. …under the laced cord (in back), and through the back of the left crook. Tighten firmly.

23. Repeat Steps 17 through 22 until 0.5 inch short of desired length.

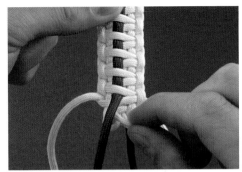

24. Pull out the last horizontal line on the lower bar.

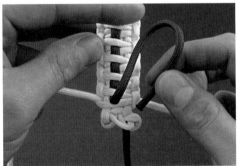

25. Then take the tip of the laced cord in hand…

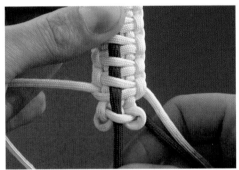

26. …and insert it through the pulled out loop.

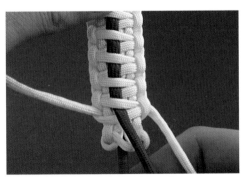

27. Flip the piece over, horizontally.

28. Repeat Steps 24 through 26.

29. Pull out the bottom right loop…

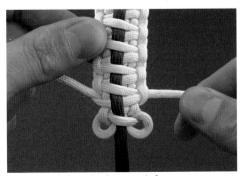

30. …and then the bottom left.

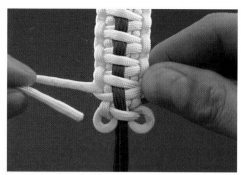

31. Take the tip of the horizontal cord protruding forward (toward you) in hand…

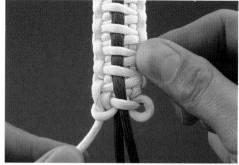

32. …and insert it through the front of its adjacent (pulled out) loop.

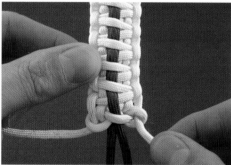

33. Follow Steps 31 and 32 in reverse for the cord protruding backward.

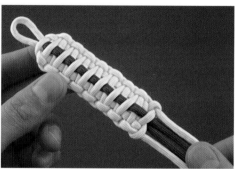

34. Gather the vertical cords dangling off the bottom of the piece…

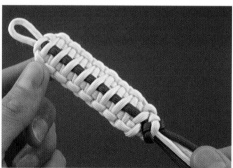

35. …and tie a 4-Strand Diamond Knot (See Page 5). To finish the fob…

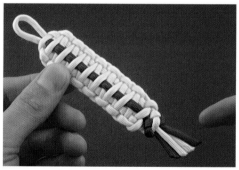

36. …carefully snip and singe the ends.

Chapter 3

Strapping
it Up

SWITCHBACK STRAP

The Switchback Strap is relatively easy to make, and is routinely one of the first pieces I show people how to tie. To add a little something extra to the strap I included instructions for how to make it an adjustable bracelet.

Cord Used: *One 6 Ft. Cord (Varying Sized Bracelet)*

Component Parts: *Historical Knot*

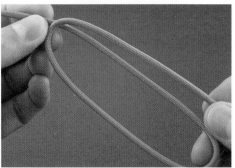

1. Five inches right of the left cord end, drop a clockwise loop the length of the desired bracelet.

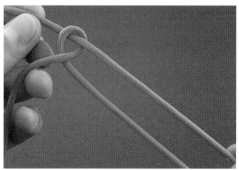

2. Hook the running end left, through the center of the loop.

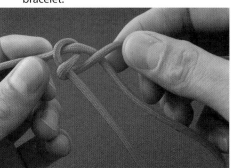

3. Then hook the running end right, and through the center of the loop, again.

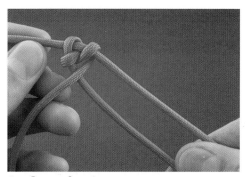

4. Repeat Step 2…

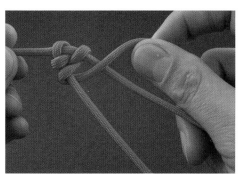

5. …and Step 3, stacking each "switchbacked" cord firmly against the one above…

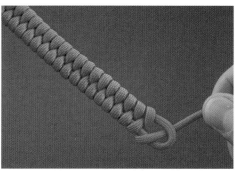

6. …until a minimum 5 inches of running end remain.

7. To firm up the piece…

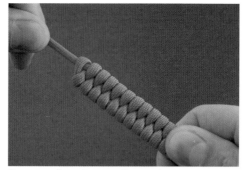

8. …pull on the standing end.

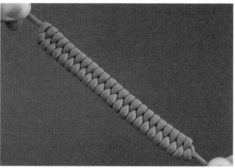

9. At this point, you've successfully made a Switchback Strap.

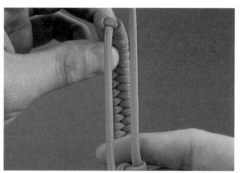

10. To generate an adjustable bracelet, line up the running ends.

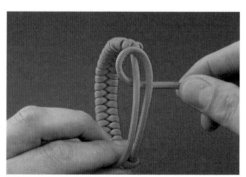

11. Then circle the right running end around the left cord and itself.

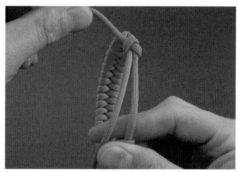

12. Insert the running end through the loop made.

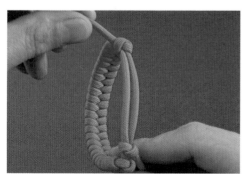

13. Flip the piece over, upside down, and repeat Steps 10 through 12.

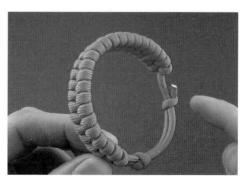

14. To finish the bracelet carefully snip and singe the knot ends.

SWITCHBACK STRAP (TWO COLOR)

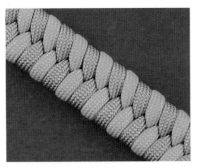

A two colored Switchback Strap is a doubling of the cord used to tie a standard Switchback Strap. However, don't be misled by this statement. There are engineering subtleties that most miss, so be sure to pay close attention to the instructions below.

Cord Used: *Two 4.5 Ft. Cords (5 In. Strap)*

Component Parts: *Switchback Strap + Doubled + Contrasting Cords*

1. Draw the two cords out side-by-side. Mark the point 5 inches right of the left cord ends.

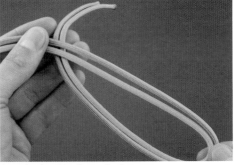

2. At the 5 inch mark, drop a counter-clockwise loop the length of the desired strap.

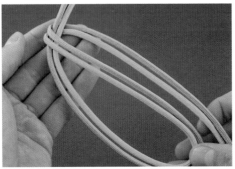

3. Hook both cord ends right, back on themselves. Then tilt the top of the piece 45° right.

4. Now, hook the outer right cord left, through the center of the loop.

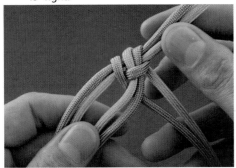

5. Then hook it right, and through the center of the loop, again.

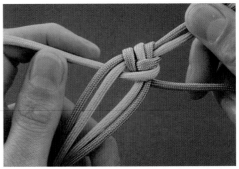

6. Hook the other right cord left, through the center of the loop.

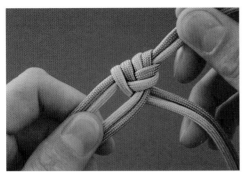

7. Then hook it right, and through the center of the loop, again.

8. Repeat Steps 4 through 7 until a minimum 5 inches of cord ends remain.

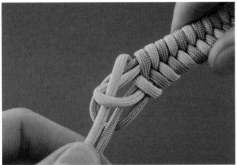

9. Insert both cord ends between the two loops.

10. Then firm up the piece…

11. …by pulling on both standing ends.

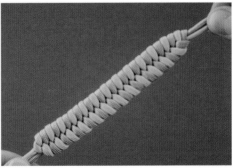

12. Once the "switchbacked" cords are set in place, your strap is completed.

STITCHED SWITCHBACK STRAP

The Stitched Switchback Strap is a slick way of adding a stitched line to the middle of an otherwise basic strap. Firm and eye-catching, the tie, like all the pieces in this chapter, makes a great strap, handle, bracelet, or necklace.

Cord Used: *One 6 Ft. Cord (4.5 In. Strap)*

Component Parts: *Switchback Strap + Stitching Technique*

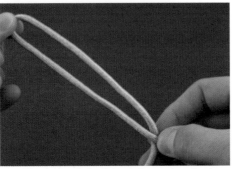

1. Five inches left of the right cord end, raise a counterclockwise loop the length of the desired strap.

2. Maintain the standing end (short cord end) on the right.

3. Hook the running end right, through center of the loop.

4. Then hook the running end left over the loop…

5. …around the left edge of the loop, and under itself.

6. Tighten the knot made, firmly.

7. Insert the running end through the center of the loop.

8. Then hook it left, over the loop…

9. …around the left edge of the loop, and under itself.

10. Tighten the knot made, firmly.

11. Repeat Steps 7 through 10 until a minimum 5 inches of running end remain.

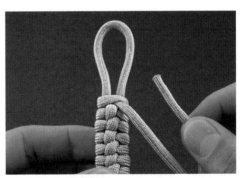

12. To firm up the piece, take the tip of the running end in hand.

13. Insert it through the center of the loop.

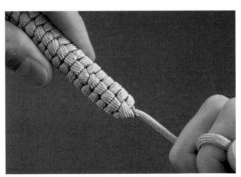

14. Then pull firmly on the standing end.

15. Adjust the stitches so that they're lined up with one another.

16. The completed Stitched Switchback Strap.

RINGBOLT HITCH VICEROY

The Ringbolt Hitch Viceroy achieves the look of the interlocking weaves of a Ringbolt Hitch in an easy to build strap—a task not readily achievable with a standard Ringbolt Hitch. Primarily purposed for a strap, the tie also makes a stylish bracelet.

Cord Used: *One 6 Ft. Cord (4 In. Strap)*

Component Parts: *Switchback Strap + Crisscrossed Stitching Technique*

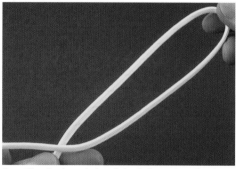

1. Five inches right of the left cord end, raise a clockwise loop the length of the desired strap.

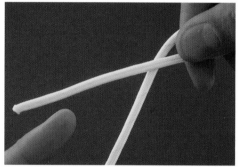

2. Maintain the standing end (short cord end) on the left.

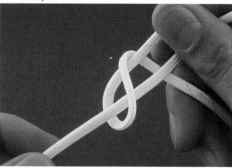

3. Hook the running end up, over, and around the loop…

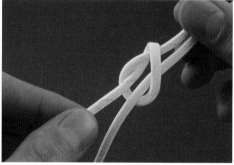

4. …then through the loop and under itself, making a "loop around a loop" or a Slip Knot.

5. Tighten the piece until firm.

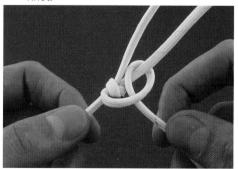

6. Now, hook the running end right, around the right edge of the loop, and under itself.

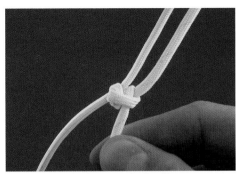

7. Tighten the knot made, firmly.

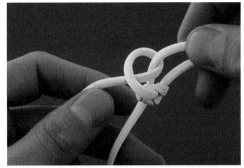

8. Hook the running end left, around the left edge of the loop, and under itself.

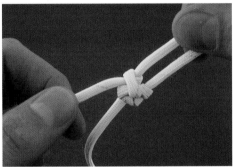

9. Tighten the knot made, firmly.

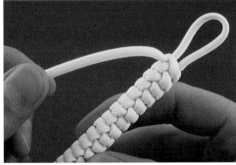

10. Repeat Steps 6 through 9 until a minimum 5 inches of running end remain.

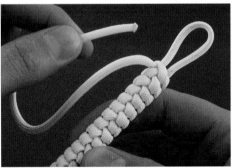

11. To firm up the piece, take the tip of the running end in hand.

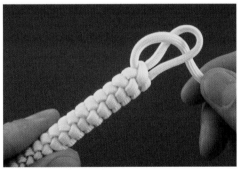

12. Insert it through the center of the loop.

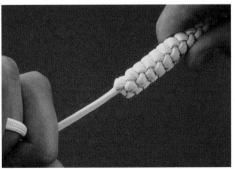

13. Then pull firmly on the standing end.

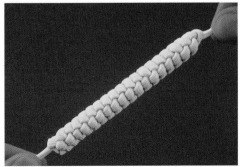

14. You now have a strap with the look of a Ringbolt Hitch!

DOUBLE-STITCHED SWITCHBACK STRAP

The Double-Stitched Switchback Strap is the logical extension of the Stitched Switchback Strap. With the addition of a second cord, it's also possible to add a second color, as the following instructions show.

Cord Used: *Two 4.5 Ft. Cords (5 In. Strap)*

Component Parts: *Switchback Strap + Stitching Technique + Contrasting Cords*

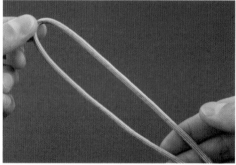

1. Left of one of the cord ends, draw out a bight the length of the desired strap, plus (+) 5 inches.

2. Hold the bight upright at the point 5 inches up from the left (short) leg.

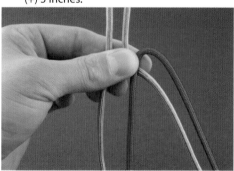

3. At this mark, line up the second cord parallel to the left leg of the first.

4. Loop the running end of the second cord left, around the legs of the first cord.

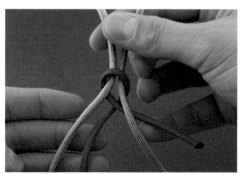

5. Then hook the running end left again, between the legs of the first cord…

6. …and up through the loop created.

7. Tighten the knot made, firmly.

8. Drop the running end of the second cord down.

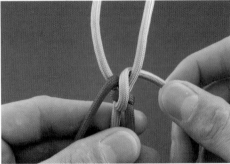

9. Insert the running end of the first cord through center of the loop above.

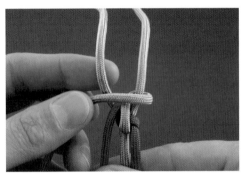

10. Then hook the running end left, over the loop…

11. …around the left edge of the loop, and under itself.

12. Tighten the knot made, firmly, pinning the running end to the right.

13. Insert the running end of the second cord through center of the loop above.

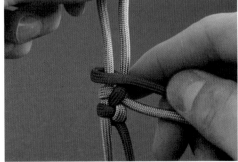

14. Then hook the running end right, over the loop…

15. …around the right edge of the loop, and under itself.

16. Tighten the knot made, firmly, pinning the running end to the left.

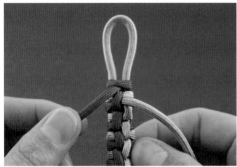

17. Repeat Steps 9 through 16 until a minimum 5 inches of running ends remain.

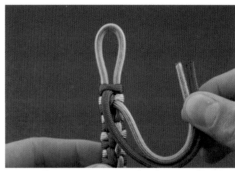

18. To firm up the piece, take the tips of both running ends in hand.

19. Insert them through the center of the loop above.

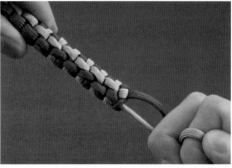

20. Then pull firmly on the standing end of the first cord.

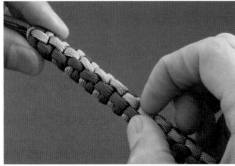

21. Adjust the stitches so that they're lined up with one another.

22. The completed Double-Stitched Switchback Strap.

Chapter 4

Endless Falls

ENDLESS FALLS

The Endless Falls tying technique is an innovative way to create a "waterfall" effect with cord. This said, the back of the tie (or the "calm" side) is equally appealing. Highly adaptable, this tie is the foundation of countless other appealing versions.

Cord Used: *Two 6 Ft. Cords (7.5 In. Bracelet)*

Component Parts: *Endless Falls*

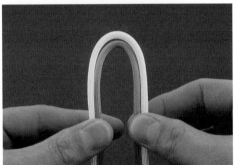

1. Start with bights created at the middle of the two cords.

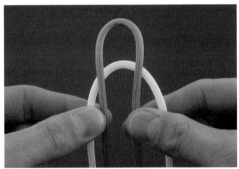

2. Drop one of the cords down 0.5 inch, behind the bight of the other.

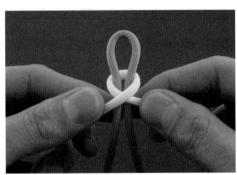

3. Cross the back cords over the front (vertical) cords, right over left.

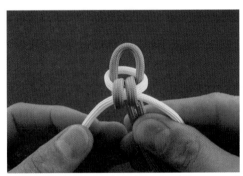

4. Circle the vertical cords around the crossed cords, between the legs above.

5. Tighten the piece until firm, leaving a 0.5 inch bight on top.

6. Now, cross the horizontal cords, right over left.

7. Circle the vertical cords around the crossed cords, between the legs above.

8. Adjust the cords until the piece is firm.

9. Repeat Steps 6 through 8 until a minimum 10 inches of cord ends remain.

10. Lock the piece in place by tying a 4-Strand Diamond Knot (See Page 5) with the loose ends.

11. Carefully snip and singe two cord ends (same color).

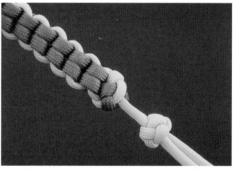

12. Then tie a 2-Strand Diamond Knot (See Page 2) with the vertical cords remaining.

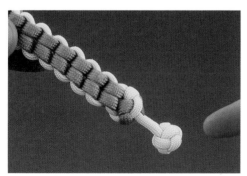

13. Carefully snip and singe the knot ends.

14. The completed Endless Falls Bracelet—falls side out.

DIVIDED ENDLESS FALLS

Divided Endless Falls unite the look and flow of standard Endless Falls with the side-by-side layout of integrated contrasting cords. The end result is striking, generating an attractive tie that's sure to catch attention.

Cord Used: *Two 6 Ft. Cords (7.5 In. Bracelet)*

Component Parts: *Endless Falls + Integrated Contrasting Cords*

1. Start with bights created at the middle of the two cords.

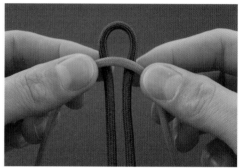

2. Drop one of the cords down, 0.5 inch, in front of the bight of the other.

3. Hook the right running end of the back cord left, over the vertical cords to the left.

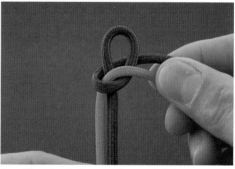

4. Then hook the running end right, around the back of the top loop…

5. …left around the front of the top loop…

6. …and through the left crook, making a "loop around a loop" or a Slip Knot.

7. Tighten the piece until firm…

8. …leaving a 0.5 inch loop on top.

9. Now, cross the horizontal cords, right over left.

10. Circle the vertical cords around the crossed cords, between the legs above.

11. Adjust the cords until the piece is firm.

12. Repeat Steps 9 through 11 until a minimum 10 inches of cord ends remain.

13. Lock the piece in place by tying a 4-Strand Diamond Knot (See Page 5) with the loose ends.

14. Carefully snip and singe two cord ends (different colors).

15. Then tie a 2-Strand Diamond Knot (See Page 2) with the vertical cords remaining.

16. Carefully snip and singe the knot ends.

17 The completed Divided Endless Falls Bracelet—calm side out.

18. The completed Divided Endless Falls Bracelet—falls side out.

Chained Endless Falls

Chained Endless Falls illustrates what a slight modification to the standard Endless Falls can accomplish. In this case, the "falls" are no longer seen, and are replaced by the familiar look of linked chains—a substantial shift in appearance.

Cord Used: *Two 6 Ft. Cords (7.5 In. Bracelet)*

Component Parts: *Endless Falls + Alternating Outside-Inside Tucks*

1. Start with bights created at the middle of the two cords.

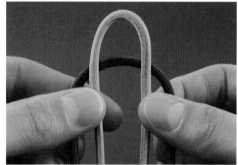

2. Drop one of the cords down 0.5 inch, behind the bight of the other.

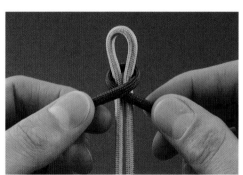

3. Cross the back cords over the front (vertical) cords, right over left.

4. Circle the vertical cords around the crossed cords, between the legs above.

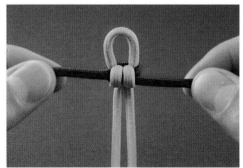

5. Tighten the piece until firm, leaving a 0.5 inch bight on top.

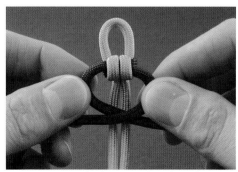

6. Now, cross the horizontal cords, right over left.

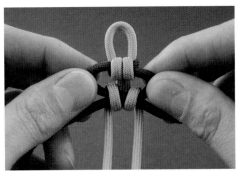

7. Circle the vertical cords around the crossed cords, outside the legs above.

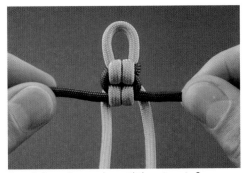

8. Adjust the cords until the piece is firm.

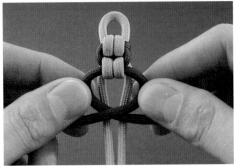

9. Cross the horizontal cords, right over left.

10. Circle the vertical cords around the crossed cords, between the legs above.

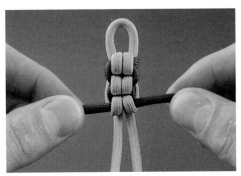

11. Adjust the cords until the piece is firm.

12. Repeat Steps 6 through 11 until a minimum 10 inches of cord ends remain.

13. Lock the piece in place by tying a 4-Strand Diamond Knot (See Page 5) with the loose ends.

14. Carefully snip and singe two cord ends (same color).

15. Then tie a 2-Strand Diamond Knot (See Page 2) with the vertical cords remaining.

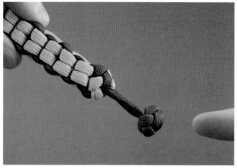

16. Carefully snip and singe the knot ends.

17. The completed Chained Endless Falls Bracelet—calm side out.

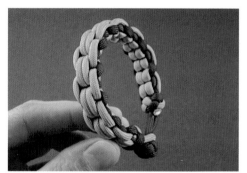

18. The completed Chained Endless Falls Bracelet—chained side out.

CHAINMAILED ENDLESS FALLS

A nod to the look of chainmail, Chainmailed Endless Falls generate a wider fall of looped cords that link together in a pattern similar to a woven mesh. Demonstrated here as a fob, the tying technique makes an equally attractive strap or bracelet.

Cord Used: *Three 5 Ft. Cords (3.5 In. Key Fob)*

Component Parts: *Endless Falls + Spectrally Clustered Cords + Alternating Right-Left Tucks*

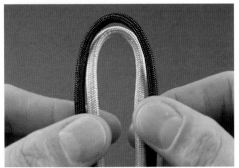

1. Start with bights created at the middle of two cords.

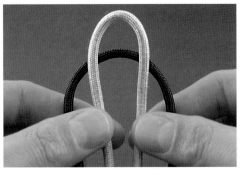

2. Drop one of the cords down 0.5 inch, behind the bight of the other.

3. Cross the back cords over the front (vertical) cords, right over left.

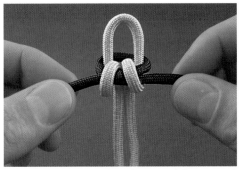

4. Circle the vertical cords around the crossed cords, between the legs above.

5. Leaving a 0.5 inch bight on top, pull the right and left horizontal cords out.

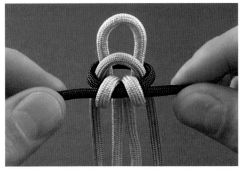

6. Lace the third cord over the vertical cords and through the loop of the horizontal cords. Stop at its middle.

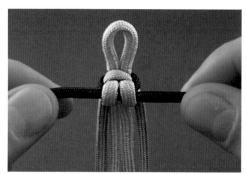

7. Tighten the right and left horizontal cords over the third cord.

8. Now, cross the front most horizontal cords, right over left.

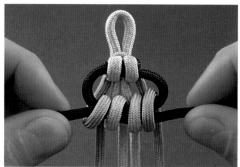

9. Circle all the vertical cords around the crossed cords, to the right of themselves.

10. Adjust the cords until the piece is firm.

11. Cross the horizontal cords, right over left.

12. Circle all the vertical cords around the crossed cords, to the left of themselves.

13. Adjust the cords until the piece is firm.

14. Repeat Steps 8 through 13 until a minimum 10 inches of cord ends remain.

15. Triangle Tie Off: Flip the piece over, upside down.

16. Hook the left running end of the horizontal cords right, over the vertical cords.

17. Hook the right running end of the horizontal cords left, under the vertical cords.

18. Hook the cord end on the right side left, and insert it through the left crook.

19. Hook the top cord end on the left side right, and insert it through the right crook.

20. Take the left cord end in hand…

21. …and insert it through the (upper) right crook.

22. Flip the piece over, horizontally.

23. Take the bottom left cord end in hand…

24. …and insert it through the (upper) right crook.

25. Adjust the tie off until firm. Then carefully snip and singe the vertical cords.

26. The completed Chainmailed Endless Falls Fob.

BRICKED ENDLESS FALLS

Bricked Endless Falls combine the standard Endless Falls tying technique with a "bricked" version of spectrally clustered cords. The product of this merger is extraordinary, generating a piece that has an eye-catching front and back.

Cord Used: *Three 5 Ft. Cords (3.5 In. Key Fob)*

Component Parts: *Endless Falls + Spectrally Clustered Cords + Alternating Outside-Inside Tucks*

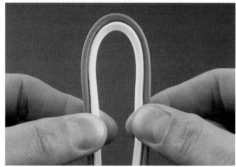

1. Start with bights created at the middle of two cords.

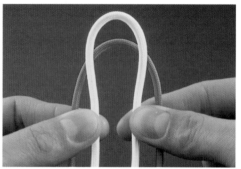

2. Drop one of the cords down 0.5 inch, behind the bight of the other.

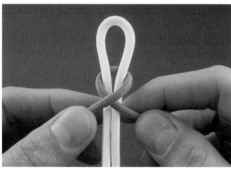

3. Cross the back cords over the front (vertical) cords, right over left.

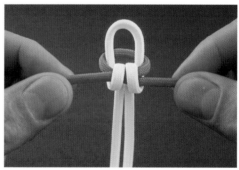

4. Circle the vertical cords around the crossed cords, between the legs above.

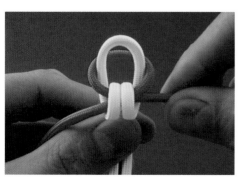

5. Leaving a 0.5 inch bight on top, pull the right and left horizontal cords out.

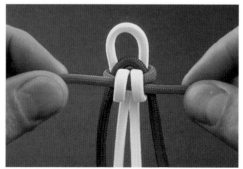

6. Lace the third cord over the vertical cords and through the loops of the horizontal cords. Stop at its middle.

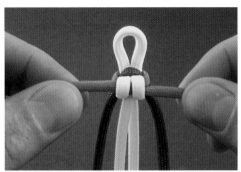

7. Tighten the right and left horizontal cords over the third cord.

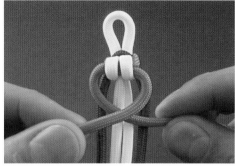

8. Now, cross the front most horizontal cords, right over left.

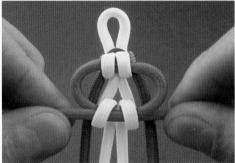

9. Circle the inner vertical cords around the crossed cords, between the legs above.

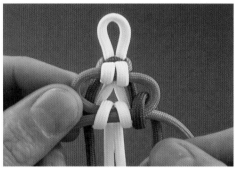

10. Circle the right and left running ends of the third cord around the crossed cords…

11. …outside themselves and before the right and left crooks above.

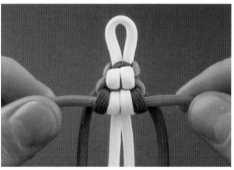

12. Adjust the cords until the piece is firm.

13. Cross the horizontal cords, right over left.

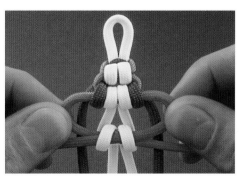

14. Circle the inner vertical cords around the crossed cords, between the legs above.

15. Circle the right and left running ends of the third cord around the crossed cords…

16. …inside themselves and outside the inner vertical cords.

17. Adjust the cords until the piece is firm.

18. Repeat Steps 8 through 17 until a minimum 10 inches of cord ends remain.

19. Lock the piece by tying a Triangle Tie Off (See Page 60) with the horizontal cords.

20. Carefully snip and singe the vertical cords to complete the Bricked Endless Falls Fob.

Chapter 5

Locked & Sliding Slip Knots

HETEROMASTUS SINNET

The Heteromastus Sinnet is a quirky looking tie that reminded me of a capitellid worm (thus the tie's name) I learned about in college. Generating a repetitive pattern that makes a great bracelet, this tie is one of my favorites.

Cord Used: *One 6 Ft. Cord (7.5 In. Bracelet)*

Component Parts: *Alternating Slip Knots*

1.   At the middle of the cord, make a clockwise loop.

2.   Bight the right running end through the loop…

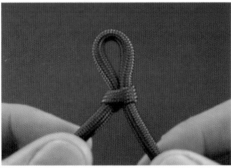

3.   …and tighten, leaving a 0.5 inch loop in the Slip Knot made.

4.   Flip the piece over, upside down.

5.   Make a clockwise loop with the cord on the right.

6.   Bight the right running end through the loop…

7. …and tighten, leaving a loop in the Slip Knot made.

8. Insert the left cord through the loop on the right.

9. Tighten the Slip Knot firmly around the left cord.

10. Flip the piece over, horizontally.

11. Make a counterclockwise loop with the cord on the right.

12. Bight the right running end through the loop and tighten, leaving a loop in the Slip Knot made.

13. Insert the left cord end through the loop on the right.

14. Tighten the Slip Knot firmly around the left cord.

15. Flip the piece over horizontally. Then repeat Steps 5 through 15 until a minimum 5 inches of cord ends remain.

16 Tie a 2-Strand Diamond Knot (See Page 2) with the vertical cords remaining.

17. Carefully snip and singe the knot ends.

18. The completed Heteromastus Bracelet.

ASHOKA CHAKRA KNOT

The look of the Ashoka Chakra Knot is sourced from the "Wheel of Law" edict depicted on the pillars of King Ashoka (an ancient Indian emperor). The technique used to build the knot is the base of multiple other ties, including the Backbone Bar.

Cord Used: *One 6 Ft. Cord (1.5 In. Dia. Piece)*

Component Parts: *Slip Knot Loop + Repeating Slip Knots*

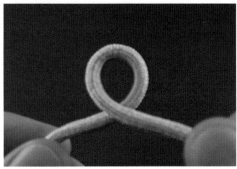

1. Approximately 15 inches right of the middle of the cord, make a counter-clockwise loop.

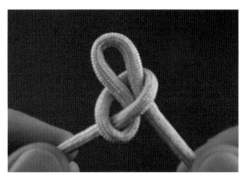

2. Bight the right running end through the loop…

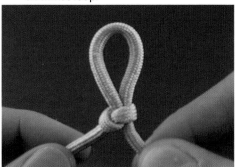

3. …and tighten, making a Slip Knot.

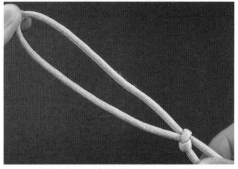

4. Pull the loop of the Slip Knot out the circumference of the desired piece.

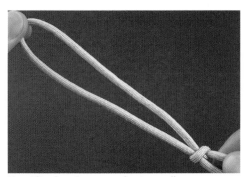

5. Flip the piece over, horizontally.

6. Make a clockwise loop with the cord on the right.

7. Bight the right running end through the loop and tighten, leaving a loop in the Slip Knot made.

8. Insert the left loop through the loop on the right.

9. Tighten the Slip Knot...

10. ...firmly around the left loop.

11. Repeat Steps 6 through 10 until desired circumference is achieved.

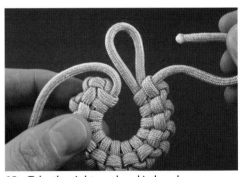

12. Take the right cord end in hand...

13. ...and insert it through the loop above.

14. Then take the left cord end in hand...

15. …and insert it through the loop above.

16. Pull on the left cord (now on the right side of the piece)…

17. …until the piece circles closed firmly. Leave the cords long for a necklace…

18. …or snip and singe the cord ends for a standalone piece.

T-Virus Sinnet

The T-Virus Sinnet calls to the mythology and imagery of the Resident Evil video game and movie series. A fusion of slip knots and cord crossing, the sinnet is deceptively simple despite its complex appearance.

Cord Used: *One 10 Ft. & 5 Ft. Cord (7.5 In. Bracelet)*

Component Parts: *Alternating Slip Knots + Crossed Cords*

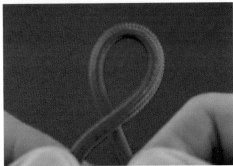

1. Approximately 2 inches left of the middle of the long cord, make a clockwise loop.

2. Bight the left running end through the loop…

3. …and tighten, leaving a loop in the Slip Knot made.

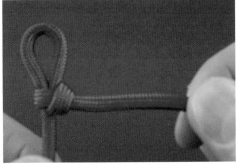

4. Two inches to the right of the first Slip Knot…

5. …make a counterclockwise loop.

6. Bight the right running end through the loop…

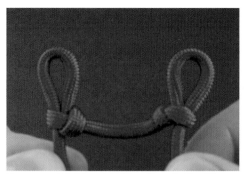

7. …and tighten, leaving a loop in the Slip Knot made.

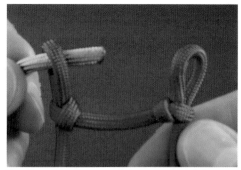

8. Lace the short cord through the left loop…

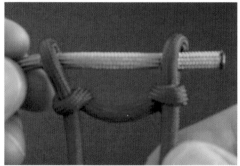

9. …and then the right loop.

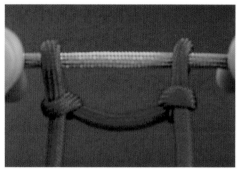

10. Set the middle of the short cord between the two Slip Knots.

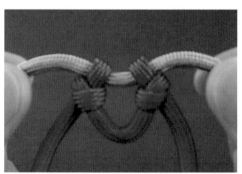

11. Then, tighten the Slip Knots firmly around the short cord, and push them together.

12. Cross the short cords, right over left.

13. Make a counterclockwise loop with the right leg of the long cord.

14. Bight the right running end through the loop…

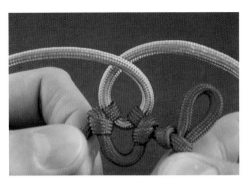

15. …and tighten, leaving a loop in the Slip Knot made.

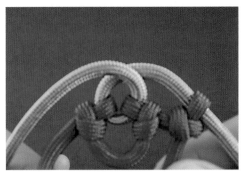

16. Insert the right side of the short cord through the loop on the right and tighten.

17. Make a clockwise loop with the left leg of the long cord.

18. Bight the left running end through the loop…

19. …and tighten, leaving a loop in the Slip Knot made.

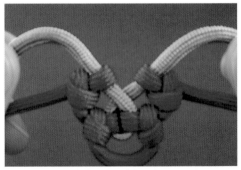

20. Insert the left side of the short cord through the loop on the left and tighten.

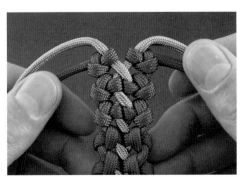

21. Repeat Steps 12 through 20 until a minimum 5 inches of cord ends remain.

22. Lock the piece by tying a Triangle Tie Off (See Page 60) with the long cord ends.

23. Carefully snip and singe the vertical ends of the tie off.

24. Then tie a 2-Strand Diamond Knot (See Page 2) with the vertical cords.

25. Carefully snip and singe the knot ends.

26. The completed T-Virus Bracelet.

BACKBONE BAR

The Backbone Bar is another demonstration of how slip knots can be locked in place to create a rigid, structurally formable bar. Evocative of a spinal column, the tie could be used to exhibit the alignment of articulating vertebrae.

Cord Used: *Two 7 Ft. Cords (7.5 In. Bracelet)*

Component Parts: *Slip Knot Loop + Alternating Slip Knots*

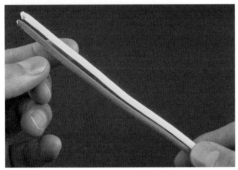

1. Draw the two cords out side-by-side the length of the desired bracelet, plus (+) 5 inches.

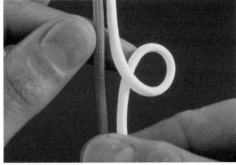

2. At the measured point, make a clockwise loop with the cord on the right.

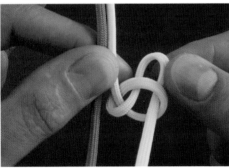

3. Bight the right running end through the loop…

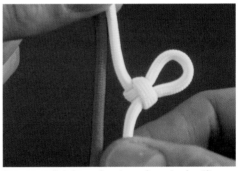

4. …and tighten, leaving a loop in the Slip Knot made.

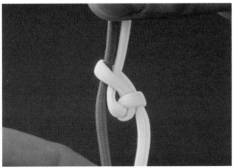

5. Insert both ascending cord ends through the loop…

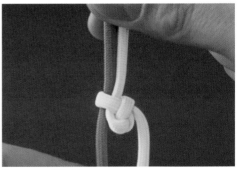

6. …and tighten.

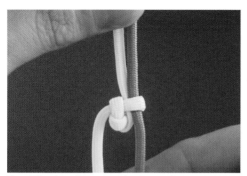

7. Flip the piece over, horizontally.

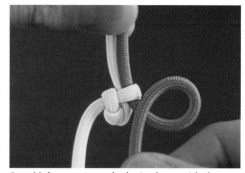

8. Make a counterclockwise loop with the cord on the right.

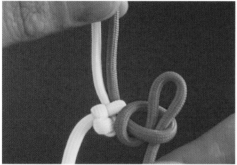

9. Bight the right running end through the loop…

10. …and tighten, leaving a loop in the Slip Knot made.

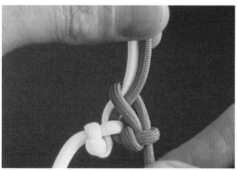

11. Insert both ascending cord ends through the loop…

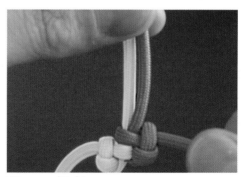

12. …and tighten.

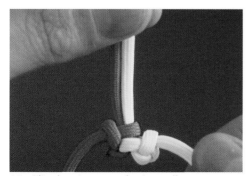

13. Flip the piece over, horizontally.

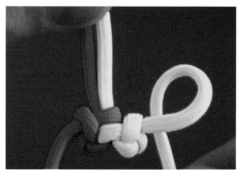

14. Make a clockwise loop with the cord on the right.

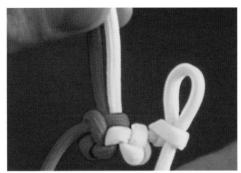

15. Bight the right running end through the loop and tighten, leaving a loop in the Slip Knot made.

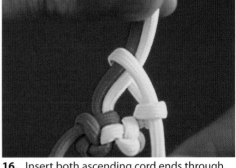

16. Insert both ascending cord ends through the loop…

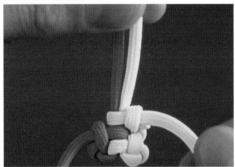

17. …and tighten.

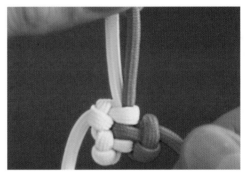

18. Flip the piece over, horizontally.

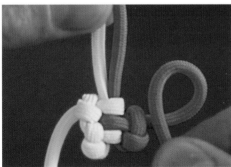

19. Make a counterclockwise loop with the cord on the right.

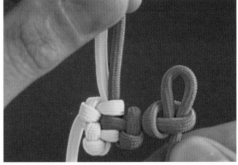

20. Bight the right running end through the loop and tighten, leaving a loop in the Slip Knot made.

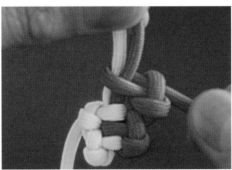

21. Insert both ascending cord ends through the loop…

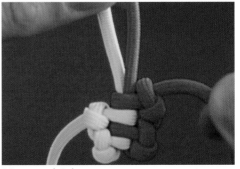

22. …and tighten.

23. Repeat Steps 13 through 22 until a minimum 5 inches of cord ends remain.

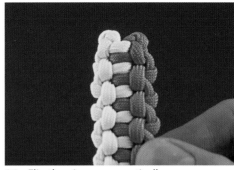

24. Flip the piece over, vertically.

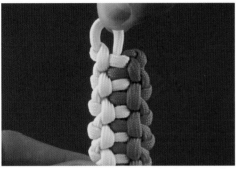

25. Pull a 0.5 inch bight out at the bottom of the bar. Then, flip the piece over, again.

26. Lock the piece by tying a Triangle Tie Off (See Page 60) with the horizontal cord ends.

27. Carefully snip and singe the vertical ends of the tie off.

28. Then tie a 2-Strand Diamond Knot (See Page 2) with the vertical cords.

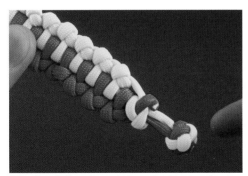

29. Carefully snip and singe the knot ends.

30. The completed Backbone Bar Bracelet.

RIPCORD SINNET

The Ripcord Sinnet is my response to those seeking a paracord bracelet that can be untied quickly and easily for emergency use. If this is what you're looking for, the bracelet below provides access to 12 feet of paracord in less that five seconds!

Cord Used: *One 12 Ft. Cord (7.5 In. Bracelet)*

Component Parts: *Zipper Sinnet + Slip Knot*

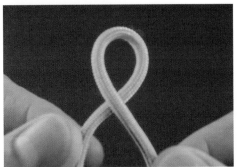

1. At the middle of the cord, make a counterclockwise loop.

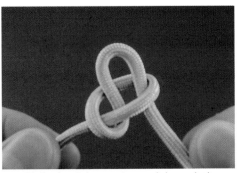

2. Bight the right running end through the loop…

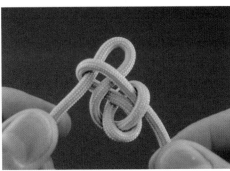

3. …then bight the left running end through the right bight.

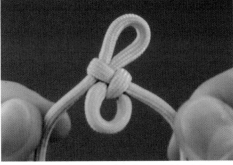

4. Tighten the piece, leaving a 0.5 inch loop at the bottom.

5. Make a clockwise loop with the cord on the right.

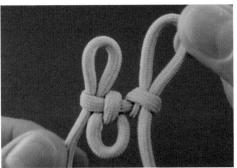

6. Bight the right running end through the loop and tighten, leaving a 1 inch loop in the Slip Knot made.

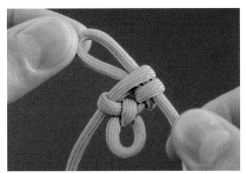

7. Insert the loop on the right through the loop on the left.

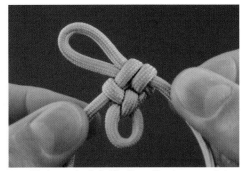

8. Tighten the left Slip Knot firmly around the right loop.

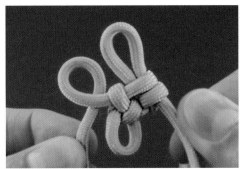

9. Make a counterclockwise loop with the cord on the left.

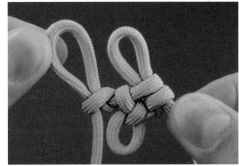

10. Bight the left running end through the loop and tighten, leaving a 1 inch loop in the Slip Knot made.

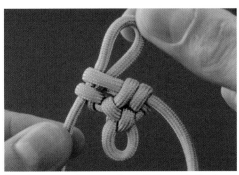

11. Insert the loop on the left through the loop on the right.

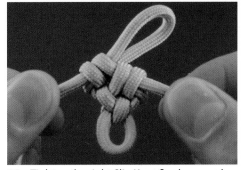

12. Tighten the right Slip Knot firmly around the left loop.

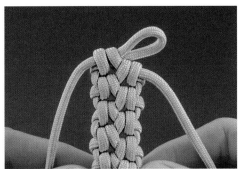

13. Repeat Steps 5 through 12 until a minimum 3 inches of cord ends remain.

14. Now bight the right running end…

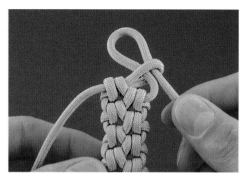

15. …through the left loop.

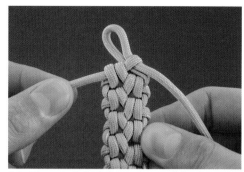

16. Then pull the left running end firmly.

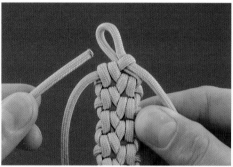

17. Take the tip of the left running end in hand…

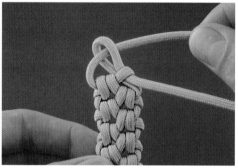

18. …and insert it through the right loop.

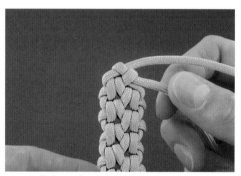

19. Pull the right running end firmly.

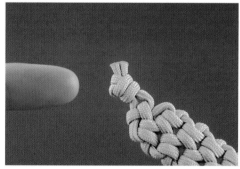

20. Finish the piece off with an Overhand Knot, its ends carefully snipped and singed.

21. Slide the knot through the loop on the other end to connect the bracelet.

22. To retrieve the cord within the bracelet…

23. …remove the bracelet from your wrist…

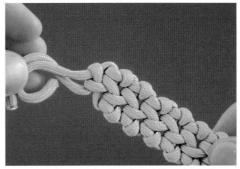

24. …and untie the Overhand Knot (clasp).

25. Then, undo the Slip Knot below the knot…

26. …and start to pull the two running ends apart.

27. Soon you'll realize why the piece is called a Ripcord Sinnet.

28. Twelve feet of paracord, from bracelet to bundle, in less than 5 seconds!

Chapter 6

Raising the Bar

SPINDLE FIBER BAR

Spindle fibers are protein structures that pull apart chromosomes during cell division. The Spindle Fiber Bar evokes the look of these helpful proteins through the repetition of interlocking hitches.

Cord Used: *One 7 Ft. & 3 Ft. Cord (7.5 In. Bracelet)*

Component Parts: *Opposing Half Hitches +*

Interlocking + Contrasting Cords

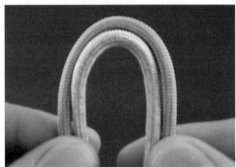

1. Start with bights created at the middle of the two cords.

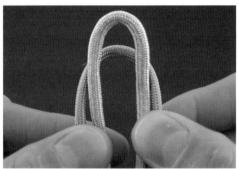

2. Drop the long cord down 0.5 inch, behind the bight of the short cord.

3. Cross the back cords over the front (vertical) cords, right over left.

4. Circle the vertical cords around the crossed cords, between the legs above.

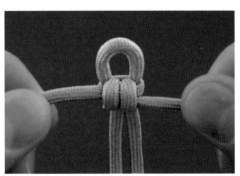

5. Tighten the piece until firm, leaving a 0.5 inch bight on top.

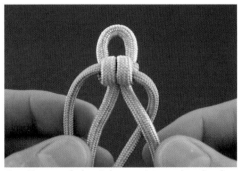

6. Now, tuck the right running end under the vertical cord next to it.

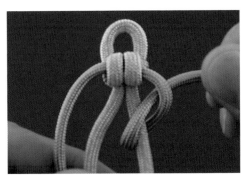

7. Then loop it around, inserting it through the right crook to make a Half Hitch.

8. Loop the left running end right, over the vertical cord next to it, through…

9. …the crook of the first hitch, and over itself, making an opposing Half Hitch.

10. Repeat Steps 6 through 9, until a minimum 5 inches of cord ends remain.

11. Now, hook the right running end left, over the vertical cords.

12. Drop the left running end over the cord beneath it.

13. Then hook it right, under the vertical cords, and through the back of the right crook. Tighten firmly.

14. Hook the left running end right, over the vertical cords.

15. Drop the right running end over the cord beneath it.

16. Then hook it left, under the vertical cords, and through the back of the left crook. Tighten firmly.

17. Carefully snip and singe the horizontal cord ends.

18. Tie a 2-Strand Diamond Knot (See Page 2) with the vertical cords.

19. Carefully snip and singe the knot ends.

20. The completed Spindle Bar Bracelet.

DOTTED BLAZE BAR

The Dotted Blaze Bar is a standard Blaze Bar tied with one continuous strip of cord over a second cord of another color. The product of this method of tying is a subtle, yet stylish dotting of color along the length of the bar.

Cord Used: *One 7 Ft. & 3 Ft. Cord (7.5 In. Bracelet)*

Component Parts: *Blaze Bar + Contrasting Cords*

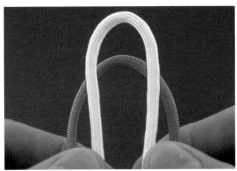

1. Start with bights created at the middle of the two cords.

2. Drop the long cord down 0.5 inch, behind the bight of the short cord.

3. Cross the back cords over the front (vertical) cords, right over left.

4. Circle the vertical cords around the crossed cords, between the legs above.

5. Tighten the piece until firm, leaving a 0.5 inch bight on top.

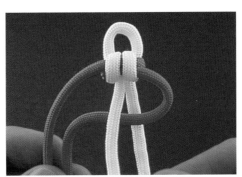

6. Hook the right running end left, over and under the vertical cords.

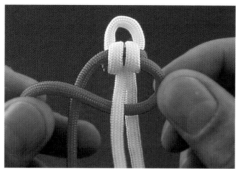

7. Drop the left running end under the cord beneath it.

8. Then hook the left running end right, over and under the vertical cords.

9. Insert the running end through the back of the right crook. Tighten firmly.

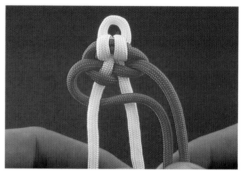

10. Hook the left running end right, under and over the vertical cords.

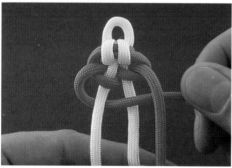

11. Drop the right running end over the cord beneath it.

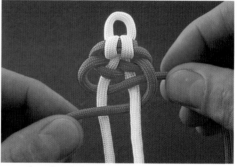

12. Then hook the right running end left, under and over the vertical cords.

13. Insert the running end through the front of the left crook. Tighten firmly.

14. Repeat Steps 6 through 13, until a minimum 5 inches of cord ends remain.

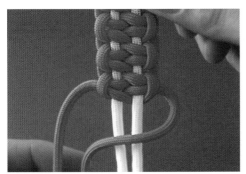

15. Now, hook the right running end left, over the vertical cords.

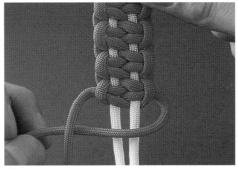

16. Drop the left running end over the cord beneath it.

17. Then hook it right, under the vertical cords, and through the back of the right crook. Tighten firmly.

18. Hook the left running end right, over the vertical cords.

19. Drop the right running end over the cord beneath it.

20. Then hook it left, under the vertical cords, and through the back of the left crook. Tighten firmly.

21. Carefully snip and singe the horizontal cord ends.

22. Tie a 2-Strand Diamond Knot (See Page 2) with the vertical cords.

23. Carefully snip and singe the knot ends.

24. The completed Dotted Blaze Bar Bracelet.

DUALITY BAR

The Duality Bar symbolizes the quality of appearing as two or in two parts. Still, like the interlocking hitches that make the bar's structure sound, what at first look to be separate, are at the same time, integral parts of the whole.

Cord Used: *Two 7 Ft. Cords (7.5 In. Bracelet)*

Component Parts: *Opposing Cow Hitches + Interlocking + Integrated Contrasting Cords*

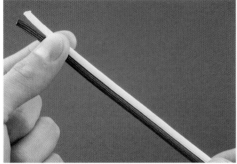

1. Draw the two cords out side-by-side the length of the desired bracelet, plus (+) 5 inches.

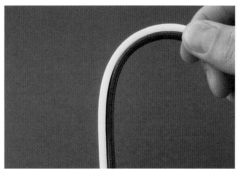

2. With the short cord ends facing down, on the left…

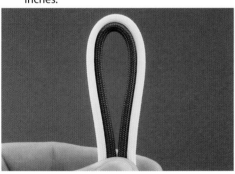

3. …bight the long cord ends to the right, at the measured point (See Step 1).

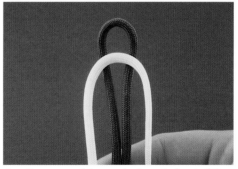

4. Drop one of the cords down in front of the bight of the other.

5. Hook the right running end of the back cord left, over the vertical cords to the left.

6. Then hook the running end right, around the back of the top loop…

7. …left around the front of the top loop…

8. …and through the left crook, making a "loop around a loop" or a Slip Knot.

9. Tighten the piece until firm, leaving a 0.5 inch loop on top.

10. Now, tuck the right running end under the vertical cord next to it.

11. Then loop it around, inserting it through the right crook to make a Half Hitch.

12. Loop the left running end right, over the vertical cord next to it, through…

13. …the crook of the first hitch, and over itself, making an opposing Half Hitch.

14. Cross the right running end over the vertical cord next to it.

15. Then loop it around, inserting it through the right crook, turning the Half Hitch above into a Cow Hitch.

16. Loop the left running end right, under the vertical cord next to it, through…

17. …the crook of the opposing hitch, and under itself, turning the Half Hitch above into a Cow Hitch.

18. Repeat Steps 10 through 17, until a minimum 5 inches of cord ends remain.

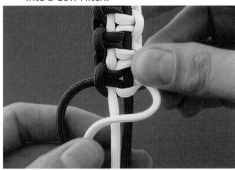

19. Now, hook the right running end left, over the vertical cords.

20. Drop the left running end over the cord beneath it.

21. Then hook it right, under the vertical cords, and through the back of the right crook. Tighten firmly.

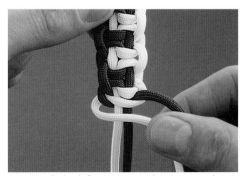

22. Hook the left running end right, over the vertical cords.

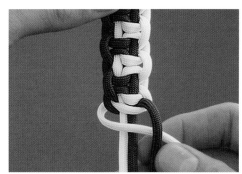

23. Drop the right running end over the cord beneath it.

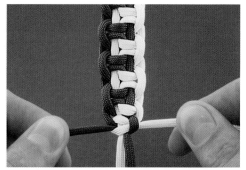

24. Then hook it left, under the vertical cords, and through the back of the left crook. Tighten firmly.

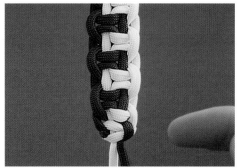

25. Carefully snip and singe the horizontal cord ends.

26. Tie a 2-Strand Diamond Knot (See Page 2) with the vertical cords.

27. Carefully snip and singe the knot ends.

28. The completed Duality Bar Bracelet.

BLAZE BAR

The Blaze Bar is so named for the fiery pattern the contrasting interlaced cords of the tie create. Taking on a finished look like no other piece to date, the Blaze Bar makes a sturdy strap or bracelet.

Cord Used: *Two 7 Ft. Cords (7.5 In. Bracelet)*

Component Parts: *Blaze Bar + Integrated Contrasting Cords*

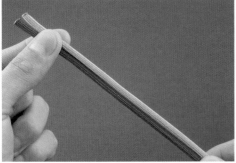

1. Draw the two cords out side-by-side the length of the desired bracelet, plus (+) 5 inches.

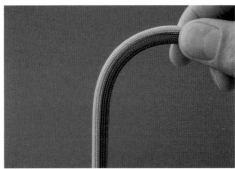

2. With the short cord ends facing down, on the left…

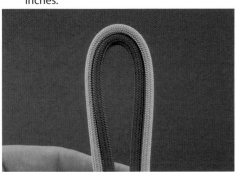

3. …bight the long cord ends to the right, at the measured point (See Step 1).

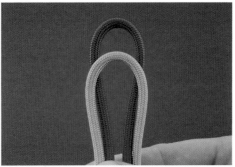

4. Drop one of the cords down in front of the bight of the other.

5. Hook the right running end of the back cord left, over the vertical cords to the left.

6. Then hook the running end right, around the back of the top loop…

7. ...left around the front of the top loop...

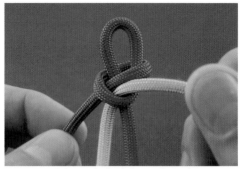

8. ...and through the left crook, making a "loop around a loop" or a Slip Knot.

9. Tighten the piece until firm, leaving a 0.5 inch loop on top.

10. Hook the right running end left, over and under the vertical cords.

11. Drop the left running end under the cord beneath it.

12. Then hook the left running end right, over and under the vertical cords.

13. Insert the running end through the back of the right crook. Tighten firmly.

14. Hook the left running end right, under and over the vertical cords.

15. Drop the right running end over the cord beneath it.

16. Then hook the right running end left, under and over the vertical cords.

17. Insert the running end through the front of the left crook. Tighten firmly.

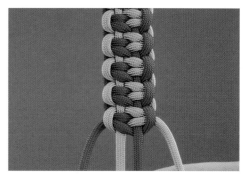

18. Repeat Steps 10 through 17 until a minimum 5 inches of cord ends remain.

19. Now, hook the right running end left, over the vertical cords.

20. Drop the left running end over the cord beneath it.

21. Then hook it right, under the vertical cords, and through the back of the right crook. Tighten firmly.

22. Hook the left running end right, over the vertical cords.

23. Drop the right running end over the cord beneath it.

24. Then hook it left, under the vertical cords, and through the back of the left crook. Tighten firmly.

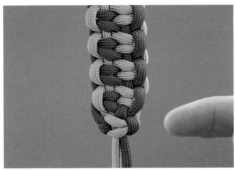

25. Carefully snip and singe the horizontal cord ends.

26. Tie a 2-Strand Diamond Knot (See Page 2) with the vertical cords.

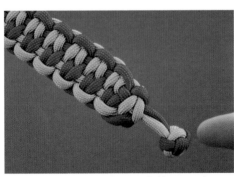

27. Carefully snip and singe the knot ends.

28. The completed Blaze Bar Bracelet.

KBK Bar

The "KBK" of the KBK Bar are the initials of my muse and better half, Kristen B. Kakos. Revealed to me in a dream, the tie was first created between two and three in the morning. My thought at the time, "Wake up! You need to tie that now!"

Cord Used: *Two 7 Ft. Cords (7.5 In. Bracelet)*

Component Parts: *KBK Bar + Integrated Contrasting Cords*

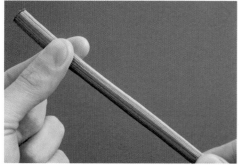

1. Draw the two cords out side-by-side the length of the desired bracelet, plus (+) 5 inches.

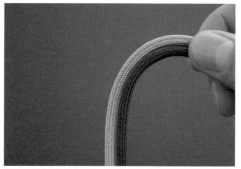

2. With the short cord ends facing down, on the left…

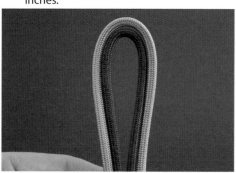

3. …bight the long cord ends to the right, at the measured point (See Step 1).

4. Drop one of the cords down in front of the bight of the other.

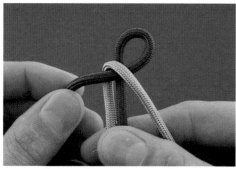

5. Hook the right running end of the back cord left, over the vertical cords to the left.

6. Then hook the running end right, around the back of the top loop…

7. …left around the front of the loop…

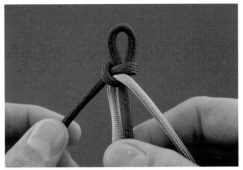

8. …and through the left crook, making a "loop around a loop" or a Slip Knot.

9. Tighten the piece until firm, leaving a 0.5 inch loop on top.

10. Hook the right running end left, under both vertical cords.

11. Drop the left running end under the cord beneath it.

12. Then hook the left running end right, over the first vertical cord…

13. …under the horizontal cord above it…

14. …over the second vertical cord, and under the right crook. Tighten lightly (not too firm, not too loose).

15. Hook the right running end left, over both vertical cords.

16. Drop the left running end over the cord beneath it.

17. Then hook the left running end right, under the first vertical cord…

18. …over the horizontal cord above it…

19. …under the second vertical cord, and over the right crook. Tighten lightly (not too firm, not too loose).

20. Repeat Steps 10 through 19 until a minimum 5 inches of cord ends remain.

21. Now, hook the right running end left, over the vertical cords.

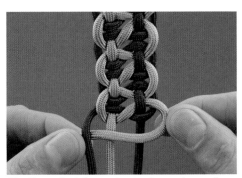

22. Drop the left running end over the cord beneath it.

23. Then hook it right, under the vertical cords, and through the back of the right crook. Tighten firmly.

24. Hook the left running end right, over the vertical cords.

25. Drop the right running end over the cord beneath it.

26. Then hook it left, under the vertical cords, and through the back of the left crook. Tighten firmly.

27. Carefully snip and singe the horizontal cord ends.

28. Tie a 2-Strand Diamond Knot (See Page 2) with the vertical cords.

29. Carefully snip and singe the knot ends.

30. The completed KBK Bar Bracelet.

Chapter 7

Back-to-Back Bars

BACK-TO-BACK BAR

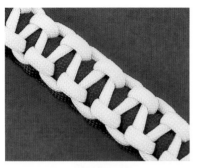

The Back-to-Back Bar is an innovative tying technique that lends itself to a variety of other ties, making it a slick way to expand the look of multiple previously established ties. Simply put, nearly every tie I've ever shown can be "back-to-backed".

Cord Used: *Two 6 Ft. Cords (3.5 In. Key Fob)*

Component Parts: *Back-to-Back + Solomon Bar*

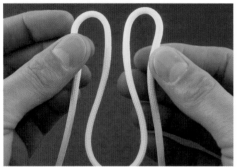

1. With the first cord, draw out a bight the length of the desired fob plus (+) 1 inch.

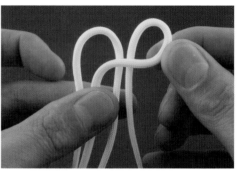

2. Hook the right running end left, over the vertical cords.

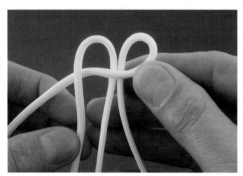

3. Drop the left running end over the cord beneath it.

4. Then hook it right and through the back of the right loop.

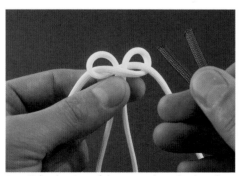

5. Take the tips of the second cord in hand…

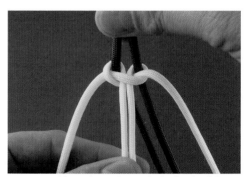

6. …and lace them through the back of the top loops.

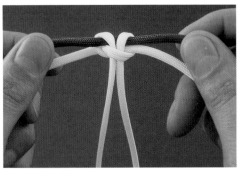

7. Stop lacing when the middle of the second cord is reached. Tighten firmly.

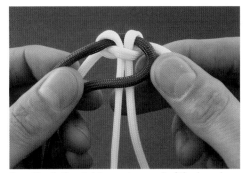

8. Hook the right running end of the laced cord left, over the vertical cords.

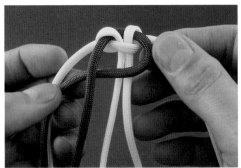

9. Drop the left running end over the cord beneath it (same color).

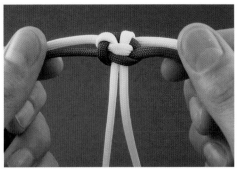

10. Then hook it right, under the vertical cords, and through the back of the right crook. Tighten firmly.

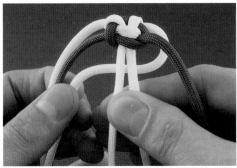

11. Hook the right running end of the first cord left, under the vertical cords.

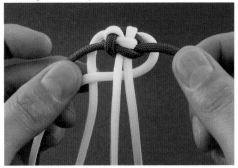

12. Drop the left running end under the cord beneath it (same color).

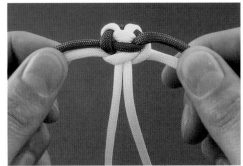

13. Then hook it right, over the vertical cords, and through the front of the right crook. Tighten firmly.

14. Hook the right running end of the laced cord left, under the vertical cords.

15. Drop the left running end under the cord beneath it (same color).

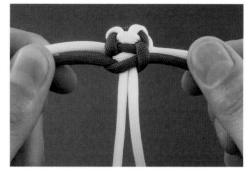

16. Then hook it right, over the vertical cords, and through the front of the right crook. Tighten firmly.

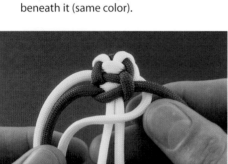

17. Hook the right running end of the first cord left, over the vertical cords.

18. Drop the left running end over the cord beneath it (same color).

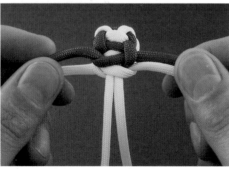

19. Then hook it right, under the vertical cords, and through the back of the right crook. Tighten firmly.

20. Repeat Steps 8 through 19 until desired length is achieved.

21. To finish the fob, carefully snip and singe the horizontal cord ends.

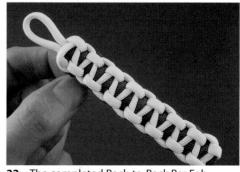

22. The completed Back-to-Back Bar Fob— back side showing.

THE WRAPTURE

The Wrapture is the corkscrew or twisted version of the Back-to-Back Bar. Its name is derived from its wrapped look and the date of its creation, May 21, 2011 (check the internet for details).

Cord Used: *Two 6 Ft. Cords (3.5 In. Key Fob)*

Component Parts: *Back-to-Back + Solomon Bar + Twisted*

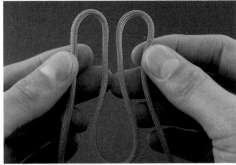

1. With the first cord, draw out a bight the length of the desired fob plus (+) 1 inch.

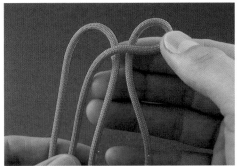

2. Hook the right running end left, over the vertical cords.

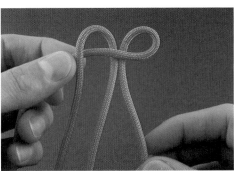

3. Drop the left running end over the cord beneath it.

4. Then hook it right and through the back of the right loop.

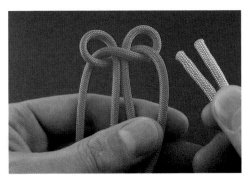

5. Take the tips of the second cord in hand…

6. …and lace them through the back of the top loops.

7. Stop lacing when the middle of the second cord is reached. Tighten firmly.

8. Hook the right running end of the laced cord left, over the vertical cords.

9. Drop the left running end over the cord beneath it (same color).

10. Then hook it right, under teh vertical cords, and through the back of the right crook. Tighten firmly.

11. Hook the right running end of the first cord left, over the vertical cords.

12. Drop the left running end over the cord beneath it (same color).

13. Then hook it right, under the vertical cords, and through the back of the right crook. Tighten firmly.

14. Repeat Steps 8 through 13 until 0.5 inch short of desired length.

15. Now, hook the right running end of the laced cord left, over the vertical cords.

16. Drop the left running end over the cord beneath it (same color).

17. Then hook it right, under the vertical cords, and through the back of the right crook. Tighten firmly.

18. Hook the left running end of the laced cord right, over the vertical cords.

19. Drop the right running end over the cord beneath it (same color).

20. Then hook it left, under the vertical cords, and through the back of the left crook. Tighten firmly.

21. Carefully snip and singe the horizontal cord ends.

22. Now sit back and soak in the Wrapture. It makes a great fob!

TIRE TREAD

The Tire Tread Bar is a subtle modification of the Back-to-Back Bar. Still, the resulting tie looks very different from its derivation, producing a rigid bar that not only looks good, but feels good against the skin.

Cord Used: *Two 7 Ft. Cords (7.5 In. Bracelet)*

Component Parts: *Back-to-Back + Solomon Bar + Drop Over*

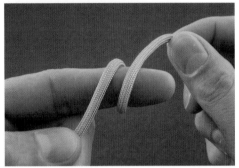

1.   Stopper Knot: Circle the middle of the cord around your forefinger once…

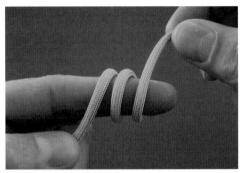

**2.   **…and then twice.

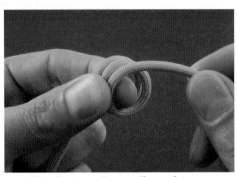

**3.   **Slide the tie to the tip off your finger.

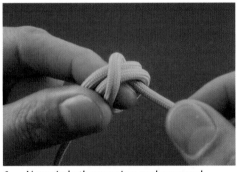

**4.   **Now circle the running end over and through the back of the coiled cords once…

**5.   **…and then twice.

**6.   **Slide the tie off your finger.

7. Take up slack in the line…

8. …until the Stopper Knot is firm. This knot will be the used to clasp the bracelet.

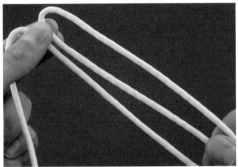

9. With the second cord, draw out a bight the length of the desired bracelet, plus (+) 0.5 inch.

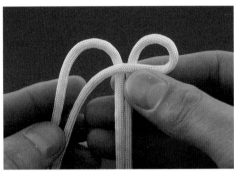

10. Hook the right running end left, over the vertical cords.

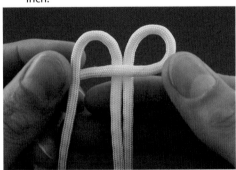

11. Drop the left running end over the cord beneath it.

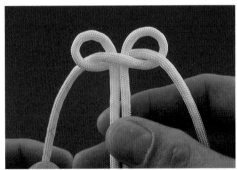

12. Then hook it right and through the back of the right loop.

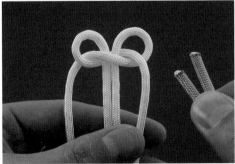

13. Take the tips of the first (knotted) cord in hand…

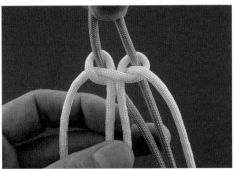

14. …and lace them through the back of the top loops.

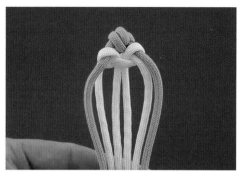

15. Stop lacing when the knot is reached. Tighten firmly.

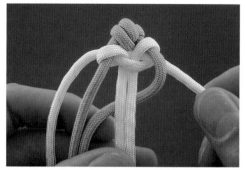

16. Hook the right running end of the knotted cord left, under the vertical cords.

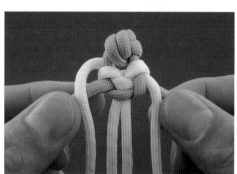

17. Drop the left running end under the cord beneath it (same color).

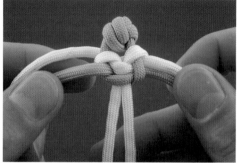

18. Then hook it right, over the vertical cords, and through the front of the right crook. Tighten firmly.

19. Drop the running ends of the second cord over the horizontal cords beneath it.

20. Hook the right running end of the second cord left, over the vertical cords.

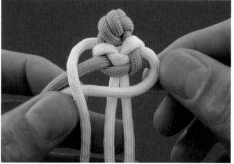

21. Drop the left running end over the cord beneath it (same color).

22. Then hook it right, under the vertical cords, and through the back of the right crook. Tighten firmly.

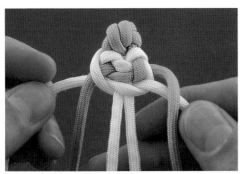

23. Drop the running ends of the knotted cord over the horizontal cords beneath it.

24. Hook the right running end of the knotted cord left, under the vertical cords.

25. Drop the left running end under the cord beneath it (same color).

26. Then hook it right, over the vertical cords, and through the front of the right crook. Tighten firmly.

27. Repeat Steps 19 through 26 until 0.5 inch short of desired length.

28. Now, hook the right running end of the knotted cord left, over the vertical cords.

29. Drop the left running end over the cord beneath it (same color).

30. Then hook it right, under the vertical cords, and through the back of the right crook. Tighten firmly.

31. Carefully snip and singe the horizontal cord ends.

32. The completed Tire Tread Bar Bracelet.

FEATHER BAR (BACK-TO-BACK)

The back-to-back version of the Feather Bar is, in my opinion, the cleanest looking back-to-back tie possible. Easily the widest tie in the genre, its brawny, dual colored, reversible nature makes a great bracelet—in effect providing two bracelets in one.

Cord Used: *Two 7 Ft. Cords (7.5 In. Bracelet)*

Component Parts: *Back-to-Back + Feather Bar*

1. Start with a Stopper Knot (See Page 112) tied at the middle of the first cord.

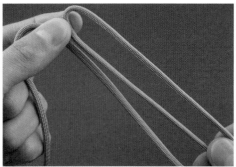

2. With the second cord, draw out a bight the length of the desired bracelet.

3. Hook the right running end left, over the vertical cords.

4. Drop the left running end over the cord beneath it.

5. Then hook it right and through the back of the right loop.

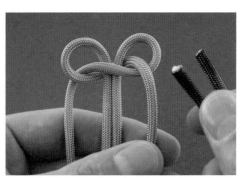

6. Take the tips of the first (knotted) cord in hand…

7. …and lace them through the back of the top loops.

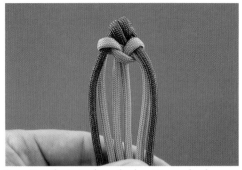

8. Stop lacing when the knot is reached. Tighten firmly.

9. Hook the right running end of the knotted cord left, under and over the vertical cords.

10. Drop the left running end over the cord beneath it (same color).

11. Then hook the left running end right, under and over the vertical cords.

12. Insert the running end through the front of the right crook. Tighten firmly.

13. Hook the right running end of the second cord left, under and over the vertical cords.

14. Drop the left running end over the cord beneath it (same color).

15. Then hook the left running end right, under and over the vertical cords.

16. Insert the running end through the front of the right crook. Tighten firmly.

17. Repeat Steps 9 through 16 until 0.5 inch short of desired length.

18. Now, hook the right running end of the knotted cord left, over the vertical cords.

19. Drop the left running end over the cord beneath it (same color).

20. Then hook it right, under the vertical cords, and through the back of the right crook. Tighten firmly.

21. Hook the left running end of the knotted cord right, over the vertical cords.

22. Drop the right running end over the cord beneath it (same color).

23. Then hook it left, under the vertical cords, and through the back of the left crook. Tighten firmly.

24. Carefully snip and singe the horizontal cord ends.

25. The completed Back-to-Back Feather Bar Bracelet—side view.

26. The completed Back-to-Back Feather Bar Bracelet—back side out.

SHARK JAW BONE (BACK-TO-BACK)

The Shark Jaw Bone (SJB) generates a pattern akin to the conveyor belt of teeth seen along the jaw bones of sharks (thus the tie's name). Tied back-to-back, the SJB is stepped up to a level of awesome few bracelets achieve!

Cord Used: *Two 7 Ft. Cords (7.5 In. Bracelet)*

Component Parts: *Back-to-Back + Shark Jaw Bone*

1. Draw the two cords out side-by-side the length of the desired bracelet, plus (+) 5 inches.

2. At the measured point, make an Overhand Knot, with the short cord ends facing down.

3. Now, hook the right running end left, over…

4. …and under the vertical cords.

5. Then, hook the left running end right, around the horizontal cord behind it…

6. …over the vertical cords, and through the back of the right crook.

7. Adjust the resulting knot…

8. …until firm.

9. Hook the left running end right, over and under the vertical cords.

10. Hook the right running end left, over and under the vertical cords…

11. …under the horizontal cord above it, and through the back of its crook.

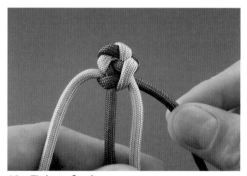

12. Tighten firmly.

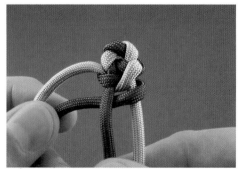

13. Hook the right running end left, over and under the vertical cords.

14. Hook the left running end right, over and under the vertical cords…

15. …under the horizontal cord above it, and through the back of its crook.

16. Tighten firmly.

17. Repeat Steps 9 through 16 until a minimum 5 inches of cord ends remain.

18. At the top of the piece…

19. …grip the tip of the right vertical cord…

20. …and pull it out until you create a 0.5 inch bight.

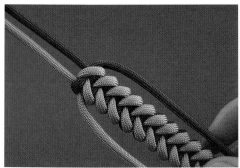

21. Flip the piece over, upside down…

22. …and tighten firmly.

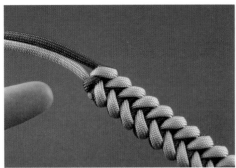

23. Carefully snip and singe the horizontal
cord ends.

24 Tie a 2-Strand Diamond Knot (See Page 2)
with the vertical cords…

25. …then carefully snip and singe the knot
ends.

26. The completed Shark Jaw Bone Bracelet—
back side out.